T0131610

GOD
IS LOVE
A Spiritual Journey from
fear to LOVE

JOYCE STEWART

BALBOA.
PRESS

A DIVISION OF HAY HOUSE

Balboa Press books may be ordered through booksellers or by contacting:

Balboa Press
A Division of Hay House
1663 Liberty Drive
Bloomington, IN 47403
www.balboapress.com
1 (877) 407-4847

Print information available on the last page.

ISBN: 978-1-5043-6607-6 (sc)
ISBN: 978-1-5043-6609-0 (hc)
ISBN: 978-1-5043-6608-3 (e)

Library of Congress Control Number: 2016915206

Balboa Press rev. date: 09/15/2016

This book is dedicated to the spiritual seekers in the world

Those who have been a part of my spiritual journey
Those who were not
afraid to ask me the difficult questions
Those who encouraged me to find my own path

Thank you

Contents

Acknowledgments

As a psychotherapist I have had the privilege of helping many clients move beyond fear into a place of love in their lives and in their relationships. I am grateful for their willingness to trust me through this process as we have dismantled long-held beliefs and have created a new understanding of life. These clients encouraged me to write this book so other people could live in the freedom they now enjoy.

I thank my mother, Joan Andersen; my daughter, Jill Stewart; and a special friend, my assistant Mary Anna Bays, for talking the time to read through the rough draft and the final manuscript.

I am grateful to Mary Anna for walking alongside me on this spiritual journey; for all the crazy theological discussions we have had, taking apart all that we have ever believed and examining it from many perspectives, and for being willing to think outside the box with me, asking many questions and contributing powerful insights.

I thank God, the Holy Spirit, and Jesus for taking me on this journey of faith and for helping me to identify my fears and to understand what "God is love" means for me.

Introduction

God is love. I encountered this phrase throughout my life in what I read, in what I was taught in church, and in what people shared with me. I thought I had a good understanding of what it meant. However, that certainty began to change a number of years ago when God asked me if I would be willing to surrender everything I believed about Him and to start over. Since I love a good challenge I agreed to this one. I realized that up until this point, I had been living my life the way most of us do: acting, thinking, feeling, and believing as church, society, media, and people prescribe. I was too busy raising children, going to school, and working to question anything.

Now that I am in my fifties, my children are all adults living their own lives, so I have had time to meet with God and to explore who He really is. Through this process I have discovered personal freedom: freedom from others' expectations of me, freedom from having to believe what I was told I had to believe to avoid hell, freedom to love God with my heart and my mind, and freedom to make decisions based on what the Holy Spirt tells me without needing the approval of a pastor, a friend, or a family member. Freedom to be me.

My spiritual orientation is Christian. I was raised in a Christian home and have attended churches of different denominations my entire life. I am not a theologian and have never attended Bible school or seminary. My intention in writing this book is not to prove everyone wrong or to defend what I now believe. What I learned came from many sources: direct spiritual revelation, personal experiences, books and media, and the experiences of others. I believe many readers will find themselves where I started—believing what they have been told to believe even though they have questions and things do not always make sense to them and being told to take everything on faith and to quit asking those questions. In the Bible Jesus asked a lot of questions, so I will continue to do that. In many churches people are discouraged from thinking for themselves as individuals and influenced to think as a group. Fear is instilled if they do not believe the perceived truth. Jesus often spoke in parables and encouraged people to look within themselves for answers rather than giving them all the same solutions.

This book is about the spiritual journey on which God has led me and about all the adjustments I have had to make concerning my belief systems and my relationships. It is a series of short essays on an assortment of topics the Holy Spirit presented to show me where my beliefs, thoughts, and behaviors had been motivated by fear rather than by love. I cover a wide range of subject matter, so there should be something for everyone in this book. Here is a brief description of each chapter.

- Chapter 1 is about the nature of God and of love.
- Chapter 2 discusses how fear and love affect our relationships with God, self, and others.
- Chapter 3 is about how fear and love influence everything around and within us.
- Chapter 4 looks at how fear rather than love motivates some of our beliefs and our church life.
- Chapter 5 is about how fear and love influence our understanding of Jesus.
- Chapter 6 looks at the fears that prevent us from going outside the Bible or the Christian faith for spiritual understanding and what we can learn from other sources.
- Chapter 7 is about how fear affects our belief systems and keeps us locked into doctrines that are not based in love.
- Chapter 8 looks at how fear limits our understanding of the spiritual realm and of everything it contains.

Some of you will read this book and decide I could not possibly be a Christian and perhaps have been deceived by the Devil. Others will read this book and find themselves resonating with some but not all of what I share. A few will strongly connect with this book, reading it repeatedly, wondering if they can find the courage to take a similar journey into their own fears and belief systems. This book is about my personal spiritual journey, and how readers respond to it will be their own personal journeys.

God is love. That may not mean what some think it means.

Chapter 1

Who Is God?

Many of you were raised to be fearful of God, believing God would punish you if you disobeyed any of the laws you were told to obey. A God who is love may be a concept that is difficult to comprehend. In this chapter I will discuss who I believe God is, what love is, and how you can love, spend time with, and clearly hear from God so you can have a loving relationship with the One who loves you.

God

Before we can talk about God being love, we first have to establish who or what God is. God has many different names depending on your spiritual orientation. Some of the more common are:

- Love
- Abba
- Source
- Creator
- Yahweh
- Great Spirit
- Divine being
- Higher power
- Universal energy
- The man upstairs

The Bible includes 364 names that attempt to describe who God is. I do not think we will ever fully comprehend all that God is until we are living on the other side of this physical world. The Bible talks about God being omnipresent, existing at the same time in both the physical and the spiritual realms. It talks about God being omniscient, knowing everything there is to know in both realms, and about God being omnipotent—all-powerful and able to do anything. God is expansive, influencing both multi-universes and individual people. There is no way any one person or one religion can define all of who God is. Today, this is my definition of God, but it is subject to change as I continue to grow in my understanding of God.

While God is the energy force that creates all things and holds them together, God is also a form of pure love that we can intimately feel and communicate with on a daily basis.

Christians look to the Bible to help them comprehend God, and they believe this is the only true source of information about him. I no longer believe this. To identify the Bible as the only source of all spiritual truth and of understanding about God and the spiritual realm seems very limiting to me. The God I believe in is much too big to fit into one book.

We each try to make sense of God based on our perceptions, our religious upbringing, and our life experiences. The problem is that once we do this we sometimes insist everyone else concur with us, in effect making God into an idol in our own image. If we can convince enough people to agree with us, we feel better. We feel like we have it figured out and no longer have to worry about being wrong in our understanding of God. I have discovered that as I remove these limitations on who God is, I experience more of who he is.

We can understand and experience God through our intellect, emotions, spirit, and physical body. God is energy expressed in many forms, communicating to all of his creation. Anyone who has had at least one supernatural or spiritual experience realizes there is more to life than this earthly existence. Such people see clearly that there is a loving spiritual force in the universe that is deeply attached to humankind, holding everything together and wanting to communicate with us. God is a relational being and has planted within each one of us a desire to reconnect with him.

People look to many things to fill up the emptiness they feel and that only a relationship with God can permanently fill. The Bible teaches that if we seek God we will find him; he wants to make his presence known to us. Therefore, I challenge you to ask God to reveal himself to you in a way or a form that you can understand and connect with. Some of the ways in which God does this are through:

- Sacred texts.
- Dreams and visions.
- Historical and archaeological evidence.
- Out-of-body or near-death experiences.

- Miraculous healing, provision, or protection.
- Complexity of nature and the human body.

While most people refer to God as Father, I believe God is a combination of both genders. God said he created us in his image, male and female. God will sometimes describe himself as giving birth to something or comforting someone.

- "So God created man in his own image, in the image of God he created him; male and female he created them" (Genesis 1:27).
- "You whom I have upheld since you were conceived, and have carried since your birth" (Isaiah 46:3).
- "As a mother comforts her child so will I comfort you" (Isaiah 66:13).

We refer to God as a "he" because it is socially and culturally acceptable and because that is how most of us have been raised to view God. Some, myself included, refer to the Holy Spirit as the feminine expression of God just as I see Jesus as the male expression of God. While groups of people are working on gender-neutral pronouns for the English language, there is not yet an agreed-upon gender-neutral word to describe God.

"God is to me that creative force, behind and in the universe, who manifests Himself as energy, as life, as order, as beauty, as thought, as conscience, as love" (Henry Sloane Coffin).

Love

As I have studied the Bible over the years, I have found that the one description of God that is most prevalent and seems to describe God best is love. Here are the major themes in the Old and the New Testaments concerning God's love.

- In the Old Testament God's love was conditional, based on the people keeping his commandments (Deuteronomy 11).
- In the New Testament God's love was unconditional. God sent Jesus to teach us about love and how to find our way back to God (John 3:16, 1 John 4:7–11).
- Today, God's love is poured into us through the Holy Spirit (Romans 5:15).
- God's love for us is unfailing and endures forever (Psalm 100:5, 109:26).
- God is compassionate, gracious, forgiving, slow to anger, and abounding in love and faithfulness (Exodus 34:6, Psalm 103:8).
- God's love is shown through his righteousness and justice (Psalm 89:14).
- God abounds in love, which reaches to the heavens (Psalm 36:5, 57:10).
- Nothing can separate us from God's love for us (Romans 8:39).

I will use the belief that God is love as the foundation for this book and examine how God's unconditional love reveals itself through our beliefs, our relationships, and the way we live our everyday lives. More than six hundred verses in the Bible refer to love, which indicates to me that love is an important concept to God. These verses talk about God's love for us and how we are to love God, self, and others.

Many people feel emotionally empty and believe if they could find someone to love them, this feeling would go away and life would be wonderful. Therefore, they look for other people to make them happy and fulfilled. They bounce between relationships or give up and settle for an unhealthy relationship. They live life from a backward orientation, looking first to people rather than to God for love. Jesus gave us the solution to this problem when he condensed every law ever written into one law, the law of love. "Love the Lord your God with all your heart and with all your soul and with all your mind and with all your strength. The second is this: Love your neighbor as yourself. There is no commandment greater than these" (Mark 12:30–31).

I believe that before we were born on planet Earth our spirits and souls lived in the presence of God and communed with God. While we have no conscious memory of this, the memory is locked away in our subconscious minds, and our spirits yearn to reconnect to their source. This accounts for our feelings of emptiness or disconnectedness. This is why Jesus encouraged us to reestablish our relationship with God. When we do that, the emptiness we had previously felt is replaced with God's eternal, unconditional love. Our spirits are reconnected through the Holy Spirit, and we are then able to love God in return. We can now see ourselves from God's perspective, receive his forgiveness, and learn how to love ourselves. When we are full of love for God and self, we have love to give to our neighbor. We can give to others only what we have first received for ourselves. We are now able to have healthy relationships because they come from a place of love within us rather than from a place of fear, need, or lack.

While studying the subject, I was surprised at how many times in the Bible we are commanded to love. And this does not mean "I will love if I feel like it" or "if you do what I want" or "if you are nice to me."

- "A new command I give you: Love one another. As I have loved you, so you must love one another. By this all men will know that you are my disciples, if you love one another" (John 13:34–35). See also Deuteronomy 11:1, 22 and 30:16,

20; Joshua 22:5; John 14:15, 21–24, 15:9–14; 1 John 2:5, 3:23, 5:3, and 2 John 1:5–6.
- "Let no debt remain outstanding, except the continuing debt to love one another, for he who loves his fellow man has fulfilled the law" (Romans 13:8). See also Galatians 5:13–14.

So what does love look like? Is it possible to define it? Here is how the Bible describes love.

- Love is sympathetic, compassionate, humble, patient, kind, joyful, peaceful, forbearing, good, faithful, gentle, enduring, never fails, does not envy, does not boast, and is not proud (1 Corinthians 13:1–8, Galatians 5:22).
- Love pursues righteousness and justice (Proverbs 21:21).
- Love is self-controlled, upright, holy, and disciplined (Titus 1:8).
- Love does not delight in evil but rejoices in the truth because love is truth (1 Corinthians 13:6).
- Love abounds more and more in knowledge and in depth of insight (Philippians 1:9).
- Love is being one in spirit and in mind (Philippians 2:2).
- Love comes from a pure heart, a good conscience, and a sincere faith (1 Timothy 1:5).
- Love obeys the commands of God (2 John 1:6).
- Love is the absence of fear (2 Timothy 1:7).
- Love is who God is (1 John 4:8).

It is easy to pretend to love. We can go through the motions and simulate these traits of love to make people and God think we love them and even deceive ourselves in the process. However, God looks at our hearts, at the intentions and motivations behind our actions and words. Do I love this person because I want something from him? Do I fear something bad will happen if I do not love him? Do I want the prestige that comes with being associated with this person? Do I feel pressured by others to love him? The Bible teaches that if our motives are not pure, coming from a place of genuine love, we are like a clanging cymbal.

I appreciate the law of love that Jesus taught and demonstrated throughout his life, because it fulfills all the other laws in the Bible. And yet I find many people continue to live by laws, legalisms, and fear. Once I experienced what it was like to live from love rather than from fear, I felt so much more freedom and peace. As God's creations we are born in the image of God, which is love. This love can be diminished or hidden, but it can never be destroyed since it is the energetic essence of who God is within us.

Love is patient, love is kind. It does not envy, it does not boast, it is not proud. It is not rude, it is not self-seeking, it is not easily angered, it keeps no record of wrongs. Love does not delight in evil but rejoices with the truth. It always protects, always trusts, always hopes, always perseveres. Love never fails. I Corinthians 13:4-8

Loving God

When you believe that God is love and that there is no fear in God, it is much easier to love him. Loving God with all your heart, soul, mind, and strength (Mark 12:30) means to love God with everything in you. But why should you love God in the first place? If you view God as being angry or punitive, it makes sense that you would not want to love him. This is why it is important to have an accurate understanding of who God is.

We love God in response to God's love for us, much like children who feel loved by their parents want to return that love to them or like a husband who feels loved by his wife wants to return that love to her. You were created to receive and to give love. God's love is unconditional, something you will not often experience from people. Most people will love you if and when you do something they want. Unconditional love accepts and loves you just as you are. You do not have to do anything to earn this love. It is freely given. It does not matter what you do or do not say, feel, think, or do. God continues to love you. There is nothing you can do to stop God from loving you, but you can resist receiving his love. To love God is to give him honor, reverence, worship, and gratitude and to live a life that allows others to see God's love in and through you. Here are some ways you can do this.

- Receive God's love for you with no strings attached.
- Place your relationship with God above all other relationships since it is out of this primary relationship that you will receive the love you need each day to love yourself and others.
- Spend time with God either on your own or in a group setting such as a place of worship.
- Keep your spirit open so you can communicate with God throughout the day.
- Spend time in nature, appreciating all the beauty God created for you, and then do what you can to keep it unpolluted and enjoyable for future generations.

- Be grateful. Spend time thanking God for all that he has provided for you.
- Look for helpful things you can do each day to bless others.
- Choose love and kindness over fear and meanness.
- Choose to offer forgiveness to yourself and others.
- Live your life by the teachings of Jesus.
- Keep your body healthy, for it contains your spirit and your soul.

When you know that you are loved by God, both on an intellectual and an emotional level, you are able to relax and to enjoy your life. No matter how chaotic life is around you, you can have peace, knowing you are safe in God's arms. The certainty of God's love removes the pressure from your relationships since you no longer have to demand love from others to feel loved. You can begin to love yourself because you realize who you are and whose you are: one of God's beloved sons or daughters. You respect yourself and no longer allow people to abuse you, because you know you are a person of great worth.

"To fall in love with God is the greatest of all romances: to seek him the greatest adventure; to find him, the greatest human achievement" (Raphael Simon).

Spending Time with God

Learning how to love God begins with setting aside time each day to meet with God, commonly called a quiet or devotional time. During this time spiritual transformation can take place from God above and from the Holy Spirit residing within you. Be open to receive from both sources, and put no limitations on when or how God chooses to communicate with you. Keeping your spiritual antennae up and on twenty-four hours a day puts you in a position to receive information, love, creativity, peace, and anything else you need at any time from God. When your behavior and your attitude are governed by fear, you clog up your spiritual energy system, making it difficult to receive from God and the Holy Spirit. This is why repentance and forgiveness are so important.

There is no particular time of day when a quiet time should take place. Whenever you choose to meet with God you want to have plenty of time and to be wide awake. People seem to think that getting up early in the morning and praying before they shower or eat breakfast is somehow holier and that God will reward their sacrifice. This kind of thinking is based on law rather than on grace. Other people believe they must commune with God at the same time every day. While this works for some people, others, especially moms with young children, need more flexibility in when they meet with God.

How long a quiet time lasts depends on how much time you have. The quality of time with God is more important than the quantity of time. Many people put restrictions on what they do during their time with God. I have found variety is best so you do not get bored doing the same routine every day. Here is a list of things you might do during your quiet time.

- Pray.
- Dance.
- Meditate.
- Sing.

- Journal.
- Worship.
- Light candles or burn incense.
- Listen to spiritually themed music.
- Read a spiritually oriented book or magazine.
- Spend time outside in nature observing and interacting with God's creation.
- Watch or listen to a spiritually oriented show on television, the Internet, or radio.
- Read the Bible to find out what it is about, to do a devotional, or to examine it in depth, using study guides and concordances.

Choose a different activity each day or each week; then you will find yourself looking forward to spending time with God rather than dreading it. Do not let guilt creep in. Everyone's relationship with God is unique, so do not compare your quiet time with anyone else's. If you cannot do it every day, God understands and will continue to love you.

"We need silence to be alone with God, to speak to him, to listen to him, to ponder his words deep in our hearts. We need to be alone with God in silence to be renewed and transformed. Silence gives us a new outlook on life. In it we are filled with the energy of God himself that makes us do all things with joy" (Mother Teresa).

Hearing from God

It is difficult to love a God you cannot communicate with. Because God is very personal, the way he speaks with you may be different from the way he speaks with someone else. As you go through different seasons of life, the way he talks with you may change, so do not put limitations on how God chooses to converse with you. Here are two things you can do to help you hear clearly from God.

Repent of sin. When people know they have disobeyed God, they have a tendency to pull away from him, believing the lie that God is angry and will punish them. Instead of running away, run toward God, repent, and receive his love and forgiveness. Sin clogs up your spiritual pipeline with God, while repentance opens it up again.

Tune out other voices. Whatever voices or messages you listen to the most will be the easiest ones to hear. The most common voices people listen to are friends, family, and media messages. The more time you spend with God, the easier it will be to identify his voice above the others, much like a child can recognize the voice of a parent in a crowded room.

Below are many of the ways God may choose to communicate with you.

God speaks through the Bible and other spiritual literature. This is the first way most people learn to hear God's voice. You get to know who God is and how he communicates with people through the stories you read about him.

God speaks through nature. All of creation reveals God to those who are looking for him, because his loving presence resides in everything he creates, not just in mankind. The cycle of seasons, planting and harvesting, death and life, the beauty of a flower or a sunset, the colors of a rainbow, and a starry night can all speak God's truth into your spirit.

God speaks through music. Listening to praise-and-worship music draws you into the presence of God where you can hear him more clearly. This can be done corporately during church or religious services or on your own by listening to music, playing an instrument, or singing to God in your home. Music can change the atmosphere of a room because it is made up of vibrational frequencies that communicate with the frequencies of our emotions, of our spirits, and of God, who holds the highest vibrational frequency of love.

God speaks through tongues. Just as God created countries, each with its own language, God created a spiritual language for your spirit to communicate directly with him. In the Bible this is referred to as speaking in tongues, and this phenomenon can manifest itself corporately and individually. In a religious service God may speak a message through someone for all to hear, and an interpreter will give the meaning. In the individual or private speaking in tongues, people speak directly to God but do not always know what they are saying. They can ask God for the meaning, and if he chooses, God will reveal it to them.

God speaks through dreams and visions. The Bible is full of people to whom God spoke through dreams and visions. A dream you will have at night while sleeping, and a vision you will have during the day with your eyes open. Usually you will know it is a God dream or vision, because it will be strong and clear and will get your attention, and you will remember the details days, weeks, or years later, or you will have an urgency to write it down or talk with someone about it.

God speaks through people. Sometimes God will speak to you through other people who will give you information about your past or present situation or may reveal something about your future that God has shown them. This is often referred to as prophesying or giving a word of knowledge.

God speaks through angelic visitation. The Bible is full of people experiencing angelic visitations. Angels can give messages from God concerning your life, because God still uses angels to communicate with people today. Some people have the ability to see angels, others sense their presence around them, and a few people are able to converse with angels.

God speaks through spirit-to-spirit communication. Sometimes you are able to sense things in your spirit, a phenomenon known as intuition. Whether it is words, pictures, sounds, impressions, or feelings, you have a "knowing" about something that came from God rather than from your own thinking, reasoning, or imagination. Sometimes it will drop down unexpectedly into your spirit, and other times it will come after time spent fasting, meditating, or seeking God.

God speaks audibly. On rare occasions both in the Bible and today, people will hear an audible voice that can be attributed only to God.

One of the questions many people have is how to discern if what they are hearing is from God or from a demonic spirit. You will know you have heard from God when:
- What you hear agrees with the teachings of Jesus.
- You feel conviction rather than condemnation.
- You have an inner peace about it.
- Another mature person confirms it.

You will know when you have heard from a dark or demonic spirit when the message:
- Causes you to experience fear, confusion, or condemnation.
- Encourages you to do things contrary to the teachings of Jesus.

Anytime you are unsure if the voice or the message you are hearing is from God or from a demonic spirit, it is best to talk with someone who is more spiritually mature or experienced in these things than you are to give you some clarity.

God is always speaking to us; the question
for us is whether we are listening.

Chapter 2

Love-Based Relationships

As a psychotherapist, I have spent years working with people in the area of relationships and I have seen time and again how much fear affects these ties. In this chapter I will address this problem by discussing the importance of loving ourselves and how this differs from selfishness, how to love others, how fear encourages competition and love encourages cooperation, how fear and love affect our understanding of marriage, and how fear often prevents us from loving those in the LGBT community. What would our relationships look and feel like if we allowed the love of God to influence them?

Loving Self

Many people do not love themselves; this is the root cause of some of their problems. Jesus taught that we could not love our neighbor until we first loved ourselves (Mark 12:31). This was a surprise to me when I studied this verse, because I had always believed that as a Christian I was supposed to sacrifice or deny myself and think of others first.

No healthy relationship can exist without first loving yourself, so let me start by defining who self is. Self is you, the unique person God created you to be, unlike any other person. There is only one you on the planet with your distinct physical appearance, personality, thoughts, feelings, desires, fingerprints, and talents. When you choose not to love yourself, you are essentially telling God that he made a mistake because you are not worth loving. Have you ever created an artwork, a recipe, a song, or a solution to a problem that you loved but others did not like it? How did you feel? Hurt, angry, frustrated, sad? Perhaps this is how God feels when you do not love the unique person he created you to be.

One of the reasons people struggle to love themselves is because they are afraid to be honest with themselves. They cover up and pretend the "bad" parts of them do not exist, so they are never free to be themselves. They fear they would be shunned by others if these parts were revealed. When you can freely admit your imperfections and not judge yourself harshly for them, they will lose their power over you. God's love can then come in and heal these parts of you.

Another reason people struggle to love themselves is because they do not see themselves as God perceives them. They think they are sinners or bad people because this is what they were taught or because of poor choices they made. However, when we receive the truth Jesus taught us, we are free, and sin becomes a choice rather than our identity. We can now see ourselves as God sees us—through the image of love rather than the image of sin.

A third reason people struggle to love themselves is because they confuse loving self with being selfish. Many people believe self-love and selfishness are the same thing when in reality they are notably different. I will compare the two.

Self-love is living life from a place of love, abundance, and peace.
- You have an appreciation and respect for who you are.
- You love and accept both the good and the bad parts of you; we are all created with the potential to do both good and bad.
- You have a sense of humor and do not beat yourself up when you cannot do everything perfectly or please everyone around you.
- You forgive rather than shame yourself.
- You are humble; you know who you are, so you have no need to flaunt it before others.
- You are teachable, able to receive constructive criticism or appropriate discipline, knowing it will make you a better person.
- You do not let other people harm, use, or abuse you.
- You live life the way you want to live instead of according to everyone else's expectations of you.
- You love yourself, so are able to freely love others.

Selfishness is just the opposite of self-love. It is living life from a place of fear, lack, and worry.
- If you do not get it first, someone else will.
- If you do not protect it, someone will take it.
- If you do not put yourself out front every time, no one will notice you.
- If you share, there could be nothing left for you.
- You put others down to make yourself look good.
- You may not want to take care of yourself, exercise, or eat healthy.

- You surround yourself with people who mistreat you, because that is what you believe you deserve.
- You are unable to love yourself, so you lack love to give others.
- You do something only if it will benefit you in some way.

If we are supposed to love ourselves first before we love others, what did Jesus mean when he talked about denying or sacrificing ourselves or thinking of others first? I believe he meant that God and I are one, similar to how God and Jesus are one. God lives within me. I choose to let go and to deny myself of selfishness, fear, lack, or anything within me that does not agree with what Jesus taught and lived. As I deny and empty myself of the fear-based things the world values, I fill the empty space left behind with the presence and the character of God. By denying myself of everything that is not love, I become love. I am now able to deny, sacrifice self, or put others before self but to do so from a place of love rather than fear.

When I am filled with love from and for God and love for self, I can give away possessions, money, information, wisdom, and time to help others and still feel fulfilled rather than depleted. The more I give away from a place of love, the more I receive back from God and others. When I deny, sacrifice, or put others before myself from a place of fear, I feel angry, anxious, cheated, resentful, or depleted.

If you have struggled to love yourself or maybe were never given permission to love yourself, I invite you to do so now. Every time you pass a mirror, stop and look at yourself and say, "I love myself and God loves me too just as I am." Some of you will have a difficult time doing this. Ask God to show you how he perceives you, and over time it will get easier for you to love yourself.

"There are two basic motivating forces: fear and love. When we are afraid, we pull back from life. When we are in love, we open to all that life has to offer with passion, excitement, and acceptance. We need to learn to love ourselves first, in all our glory and our

imperfections. If we cannot love ourselves, we cannot fully open to our ability to love others or our potential to create. Evolution and all hopes for a better world rest in the fearlessness and openhearted vision of people who embrace life" (John Lennon).

Free to Be You

Once you are able to love yourself, you have the freedom to be yourself, something few people are able to do. Why is it so hard to be you? Could it be that most people have no idea of who they really are? So many people live their lives trying to please others to earn love or approval. They believe the lie that if they can look and act like everyone else, wear the right label, live in the right neighborhood, make enough money, or hang out with the right people, they will be happy, loved, and at peace. They look to celebrities, sports figures, or the popular person at school or work to define who they are, what they drive, and what music they listen to. They look to the media and allow what they see and hear on television, the Internet, movies, or books influence how they feel about themselves. They play the comparison game and can always find someone better-looking, with a better job, making more money, or with a better-looking man or woman.

Who makes up these rules? Why is it that those who buck the system and choose to be different get bullied and made fun of? Why do we as parents stress conformity over uniqueness with ourselves and with our children?

People often confuse their identities with their roles in life. Your identity is what God says you are. Your role is how you live out this identity—i.e., spouse, parent, child, friend, athlete, musician, or professional. Your identity and value cannot be based solely on what others think of you, because their thoughts and feelings toward you can change by the hour, day, or week. If you judge yourself by what others think, your self-worth goes up and down like a yo-yo, and you struggle to consistently feel stable or peaceful. You are kept on this emotional roller coaster by fear of what others will say or think about you. If you are different, if you do not conform, if you do not agree, if you choose to look, act, think, or believe differently, you could be rejected rather than loved. You become a people pleaser. You focus on what you think you will lose rather than on what you will gain my being yourself. Loving self is learning how to stand up for you and confidently be the person God created you to be even when others may not like or love you.

To live out your authentic self, it helps to understand the difference between self-worth and self-image. While these may sound similar, they are quite different. Self-worth comes from within, having a strong, loving connection to your creator God and having been lovingly affirmed by your parents or other adults. The words people speak over you can breathe life or death into how you feel about yourself. Surround yourself with family, friends, coworkers, and others who validate and encourage you with their positive, loving words and actions. What you value in your life affects how you feel about yourself. When you value things like love, trust, faithfulness, honesty, helping others, or improving yourself, you will make decisions based on these positive values, increasing your love for self.

Self-image is how you want others to think about you. It comes from the outside, from how you package and market yourself. You seek after things and relationships that make you appear to be someone other than who you really are. If you have poor self-worth, you may try to hide it behind self-image so no one will ever find out who you really are, because if others knew that, they might reject you. However, in doing this, you lose touch with your real self, and over time you may feel anxious, depressed, angry, or frustrated. Or you may project these feelings outward at others through violent acts. You will feel the greatest peace when your self-worth and self-image are in alignment with your true self.

As you begin to receive God's love, you will be able to return that love to God. Then you will start to love yourself and will finally have the freedom, love, peace, and joy you have spent your life searching for. You will begin to be who God created you to be rather than what others think you should be. When you have reached this level of freedom, people will be attracted to you because they see the freedom, peace, and joy you exhibit, or they will be jealous of you and try to discredit you. Remember that those who treat you this way usually do so because they struggle to love themselves. These people want what they see in you, but they are unwilling to do what you did to obtain it.

Fall in love with who you are and embrace your authentic self. Start with something small such as wearing a style of clothes or a hairstyle that expresses who you are. Listen to music, read books, or eat food that you really enjoy rather than live out the expectations of others. You may not win a popularity contest, make the most money, or die with the most toys left behind. However, you will enjoy your life, get to do what you love, and spend time with those you love and who love you in return. And you will be free—free to be you.

"To be yourself in a world that is constantly trying to make you somebody else is the greatest accomplishment" *(Ralph Waldo Emerson).*

Loving Others

You have now read about how to first receive God's love for you and then how to love yourself. These two steps enable you to fulfill the last part of the law of love (Mark 12:30–31), which is loving others. So who are these others? The whole human race. That includes those who may have different beliefs from your own and those who look, think, and act differently than you. It means those who love you and those who do not.

We are far more interconnected than most of us realize. Everything in existence in this earthly world and in the galaxies beyond was created by God. He holds it all together through the vibrational energy of love, the essence of who God is. Everything you do, say, think, or feel creates an energy field that moves out into the atmosphere and affects everything and everyone around you. While you may think you are making a personal decision that involves only you, in reality your decision affects far more than you. It is like throwing a stone in a pond and watching the ripples move outward.

When you learn to view people as God's creation, you are able to see everyone as an extension of who God is. When you love others, you are loving the God within them. When you get mad and yell at others, you are yelling at the God within them. Whether you are the boss or the employee, your value is equal from God's perspective. You have a choice to go through life looking for ways to love, bless, and serve others or looking for ways to frighten, harm, or control others. You can view the world as divided, adopting an us-versus-them mentality, or you can choose to focus on what you have in common and to respect differences.

Sometimes you may think others are withholding things you need or want such as appreciation, help, or love, but perhaps you are the one withholding these things from yourself or others. Maybe if you make the effort to give them to others, even if you do not feel like it, you will start receiving these things in return. Jesus taught that you will receive what you give away. You need to treat others the way you want to be treated. Choose forgiveness and reconciliation over hatred and separation. You should not begin a relationship asking what you can get but rather asking what you can give. Why is it so difficult to love others in this manner?

We all enter the world as children with open, trusting hearts, believing everything is true and everyone loves us. Over time, we discover that the world is not always a nice place. None of us had perfect parents, families, or circumstances when growing up. People do and say things that hurt us. We begin to build walls of protection to defend against any more hurt. The problem is that while the walls keep us from getting hurt, they also keep us from receiving love.

It is easy to pass judgment on others. I was unaware of how much I was doing this until the Holy Spirit pointed it out to me. People do and say things, but rather than observe and state what happened, we attach judgments. For example, we notice that someone is late for an appointment, and we add statements to this observation such as:

- She is always late; she is so unreliable.
- She always thinks what she is doing is so much more important than what I need her to do.
- Doesn't she know I have more important things to do than to sit around and wait for her?
- Why can't she call and let me know she is going to be late? She is so inconsiderate.

All these judgments do is create separation between us and the other person. We feel intense emotions because an expectation we had has not been met. So rather than ask ourselves why we are letting this upset us, we become defensive, offended, or angry and blame the other person for these feelings. See if you can live one day without judging others. It is not an easy thing to do, but it is the more loving thing to do.

In working with couples and families, I have found that they each want to fix the other or they want the other to fix them. People are not projects to fix; they are people to love. The only person you can work on in a relationship is you. The pain in relationships comes from a failure to accept and to love people just as they are. Love has become conditional rather than unconditional.

When you look to others to make you happy, fulfilled, or rich or to save you from a situation you put yourself in, you put a lot of pressure on the other person that over time could destroy your relationship. You each need to learn how to take responsibility for your own lives.

Unhealed wounds from childhood are reopened in relationships. So do not blame the other person for doing or saying something that triggered your pain. Instead, seek help to be healed of your pain, and then there will be nothing left within you for other people to trigger. Your inner pain is healed through your relationships with God and with other people as they accompany you to listen, to encourage, or to give advice. Inner pain cannot be healed by external things such as a new car, more money, a different career, or a new house. These things will bring only temporary relief. They cannot heal the root cause of your pain. We all have acquired layers of pain from living that must be brought to the surface and released from us. This is what a good counselor can help you to do.

If you are in a relationship where someone has hurt you, rather than getting angry, consider thanking this person for giving you the opportunity to learn how to love. Perhaps this person took something and never returned it, said hurtful words, or dismissed your feelings. Jesus said it is easy to love those who love us but challenged us to love those who persecute us and are difficult to love (Matthew 5:44). However, if you are in an abusive relationship and have been repeatedly hurt, you must put up boundaries to keep yourself safe, and sometimes that means leaving the relationship. Remember, you are a person of great worth, designed with love by

God. You were not created for other people to repeatedly abuse you.

Everyone is simultaneously engaged in three relationships while on earth: loving God, self, and others. May all of your relationships be grounded in God's unconditional love.

The Us-versus-Them Mentality

We do not always consider how competition and cooperation affect our relationships and how one is rooted in fear and the other in love. Most of us who grew up in America were taught the benefits of a competitive mind-set. We were told that this mentality encourages us to strive to be better than we thought we could be, that it teaches us to set goals, to keep after them, and not to give up when things get difficult, that it keeps us from becoming lazy and mediocre. But have you ever considered the downside of the competitive mind-set? What other messages does it send people?

- We are valued, wanted, loved, or accepted only when we can beat out the competition.
- We must compete against everyone else to get what we want or need in life.
- We get rewarded when we win and scolded when we lose.
- Who we are is not good enough; we must prove ourselves against everyone else.
- Life becomes all about us and what we can do to succeed, and if we have to hurt people along the way, that is okay; it is to be expected.
- We view people as the enemy, instilling fear in us, so we avoid getting to know them.
- We see ourselves as separate from others.

Unfortunately, this divisive competitive mind-set is commonly found in churches, and we as Christians find Scriptures to justify it. We divide the world into us and them rather than focusing on what we have in common. We are taught to compete and to fight against people instead of cooperating with them. The church often uses warlike phrases such as "us versus them," "they are the enemy," "we are in a culture war," and "we need to pray against their efforts to defeat us." We judge, condemn, and separate ourselves from those who do not believe as we do. I struggle to understand how this perspective ties in with a God who is love. I see a lot of this mentality in the Old Testament, which makes some sense given the time period and the culture; war was a way of life and how people resolved conflicts. However, I like to believe that today we have made progress in this area; we choose negotiation and an effort to understand over verbal or physical alterations with each other. Here are some benefits of cooperation.

- We are valued, wanted, loved, and accepted for who we are, not for what we do.
- We work together to help each other meet our needs or wants.
- We feel loved whether we win or lose.
- We can celebrate who we are without having to prove ourselves against anyone else.
- We value other people and do what we can to help others, not just ourselves.
- Because we feel love toward others, we appreciate and seek to understand them rather than fear our differences.
- We live with less anxiety when we are not competing against each other.
- It is easier to trust people when we are working with them rather than opposing them.
- We see ourselves connected to each other.

One day the Holy Spirit spoke with me about how I categorize people into saved and unsaved, those who attend church and those who do not. She pointed out how I do not treat them the same and how I judge them differently. She told me God does not view people this way and neither should I. God believes in and loves them regardless of whether they believe in him. God resides in all people as light. In some, the light is barely flickering, but it is still there. When I started seeing God in everyone around me, I interacted with them in a new way, and I began to learn how to love all people without judgment. I now understand people to be in three basic categories:

- Those who have spiritual understanding and interest. They believe there is a God and are seeking to understand who God is and how to connect with him.
- Those who have spiritual understanding and interest but seek the dark spiritual world of the demonic instead of seeking God.
- Those who have no spiritual understanding and do not believe a spiritual realm exists. They say that even if there is a God out there, they have no desire for a relationship.

The challenge is to learn to love all people, to seek to understand where they are in their spiritual journeys, and then to meet them there. I do not think Jesus wanted us to become an exclusive group of chosen, lucky believers who see ourselves as better than others. And I don't think his message for us was that we are to compete against each other to get ahead in life or to prove our value to others. Let us see if in our lives, our relationships, and our churches we can find a healthy balance between the benefits of competition and cooperation. We are not here to change each other. We are here to support, forgive, and encourage each other to become all that God created us to be. Genuine love is what will draw people to seek after God.

> *When you meet anyone, remember it is a holy*
> *encounter. You are both God's children.*[1]

Marriage

Marriage is an important relationship in the church. I have done a lot of marital counseling and have learned quite a bit in the process. I have found that many marriages are based on fear rather than on love. The church puts a lot of pressure on marriages to be biblically correct. I was raised to believe it was important to have biblical guidelines for marriage since they provide a safe perimeter for the union. As long as you observe these rules, everything will be fine. If you depart from these rules, problems will arise. Partners focus on trying to meet these rules and expectations and then accuse each other of not doing what they are supposed to do according to the Bible. If you follow all the biblical guidelines for marriage you are supposed to be happy and never have a reason to consider divorce. But just as many Christian marriages end in divorce as secular ones, so something is not working.

I believe there is only one reason a Christian should get married. He or she prayed about it, and the Holy Spirit told the man or woman to marry a particular person. During marital counseling I always ask each of the partners why they married the other, and in all my years of counseling, no one has ever given me that answer. This is what I usually hear:

- I was pregnant.
- I was trying to get out of a bad situation (previous relationship, parental issues, or financial insecurity).
- I was drawn to my partner's character: the person was nice, funny, honest, trustworthy.
- I liked that we had things in common; we enjoyed being with each other.
- I thought my partner was good-looking.
- I did not want to be single all my life and was afraid no one else would be interested in me.
- I thought I could change my partner after we got married and everything would be fine.

By the time they reach eighteen, many people have accumulated years of hurt, trauma, abuse, or emotional wounds. If they have not healed from their past, they take all that baggage into the marriage, and over time it can destroy the union. Two broken people cannot create a healthy marriage. We can give only what we have within us. The partners need to heal from their pasts to create a healthy marriage together.

People get married with the expectation that it is the partner's job to meet all of their needs, and their greatest fear is that these needs will go unmet. This puts tremendous pressure on the relationship and is the source of insecurity in marriages. You insist your partner do things your way, think like you, feel like you, or believe what you believe. You find yourself doing things for your partner out of fear, obligation, or guilt. These behaviors are not grounded in love; they are based on fear and will lead to much defensiveness, resentment, and bitterness.

Only God can meet your needs. God may work through your partner to make this happen, or he may use other people. When you understand and feel how much God loves you, you can trust him to meet your needs, removing the pressure from your partner. This frees up the relationship so love can flow between you. Now you can seek to understand each other without needing to judge, accuse, criticize, manipulate, or become offended or defensive. The point is not to decide whose values and beliefs are right or wrong but to understand the reasons each of you has for your values and beliefs. Your intent is to understand, not to change, your partner. Acceptance does not always mean you like or agree with your partner, but it does mean you will not judge your partner as being wrong.

A challenge in all marriages is that people change over time, and so they should. People should not be the same at forty as they were at twenty-five. But sometimes people feel threatened and insecure when a partner goes through changes. If a partner changes for the worse, divorce may be necessary for the safety of the family. Partners often grow apart and have little in common anymore and will either divorce, seek counseling, or remain together in what I call a pretend marriage. They are miserable but will not get a divorce for fear that God will punish them or no longer love them, fear of what the church will say, fear of how their family will respond, or fear of being single. But what they have is not a marriage. They live under the same roof and give the appearance that all is well but essentially live as separate individuals, deceiving themselves and everyone else. We put greater emphasis on how many years they have been married than on the quality of their relationship. They may be legally married, but in my opinion they do not have a marriage.

I no longer define marriage by a piece of paper or a vow. I define it as a committed relationship between two people who choose each day to love, respect, forgive, and seek to understand and support each other. When conflict arises they know how to use it to bring them closer together rather than to tear them apart. They stay together because of love, not because they fear what will happen if they divorce.

Those who choose divorce are often shamed for not trusting God or for giving up too soon. As a society and as a church we have made it difficult and expensive for people to get out of bad marriages, so many will choose to stay in miserable, abusive, unhealthy relationships. Those who divorce do not make this choice lightly, and it is not up to us to judge since we have little understanding of what has taken place in the marriage. They need grace and love to go through the divorce process and to reestablish their lives.

The beauty of marriage is that it is the only relationship in which partners get to make their own rules. They make the marriage look and feel however the two of them want. However, most partners are not aware of this, so they continue to try to fashion a marriage after what church, society, friends, or books tell them to do. I have seen so many marital problems arise because partners start comparing their marriage to others or to what some book said and then try to force their marriage to meet these expectations. Every marriage is unique because every marriage is made up of

The LGBT Community

Most people know that LGBT stands for lesbian, gay, bisexual, and transgender. The church has struggled to understand this group, to form relationships with its members, and to handle them with love since we often view them from a place of fear. Growing up in the church I received the message that members of the LGBT community were engaging in sinful acts that God condemned, and because of that, they could not be involved in church. Our job was to tell them about their sin and to convince them to repent and to accept Jesus. All these sinful desires would then magically go away, and they would be normal. Then they would be welcomed at church and could serve in any capacity they wanted. We had the Bible verses to back up our position.

It was not until I was in my early forties and had gone back to college to get my social work degree that I came in contact with members of the LGBT community. Since a few of them were in classes with me, I decided it was time I heard their stories about why they were the way they were. I discovered that they were normal people, that they had had these feelings from a very young age, and that they had lived with inner torment, bullied and ostracized for not being normal. When they came out, it took great courage and they lost friends, families, or jobs because of it. I realized that as a Christian I had to rethink my response to the LGBT community.

I went back through the Scriptures to see what they had to say about this issue. I found that the Bible is opposed to all sexual immorality, not just homosexuality. This includes adultery, incest, rape, homosexuality, bestiality, prostitution, fornication, lesbianism, and lust. I found twenty-three verses about adultery,[1]

---

[1] Adultery: Exodus 20:14; Leviticus 20:10; Deuteronomy 5:18; Proverbs 6:32; Jeremiah 3:8, 7:9, and 23:14; Ezekiel 16:32, 23:37; Hosea 4:2; Matthew 5:27, 29, 32; 15:19, and 19:9; Mark 7:21, 10:11, 19; Luke 18:20; Romans 2:22, 13:9; 1 Corinthians 6: 9; 2 Peter 2:14.

nine about fornication,[2] and only five about homosexuality.[3] And the only sexual sins Jesus addressed were adultery, lust, and fornication; he never mentioned homosexuality. So if God forbids all of these acts of sexual immorality, why have we spent so much time focused on homosexuality while ignoring the other sexual sins being committed in the church? Fornication (sex outside of marriage), lust, and adultery are so common among Christians that they are considered normal and acceptable behavior today.

We need to step back and look at the bigger message God intended to communicate. God created us to be sexual beings and gave us sexuality as a way for us to express love, intimacy, and connection with someone we deeply love. I believe the real message the Bible is trying to convey is that it is wrong when we selfishly use others for our own sexual gratification, because our behavior is motivated by fear and a desire for power or control rather than by love for the other person.

Another common sentiment in church is that homosexuals are going to hell for their sexual immorality. I looked up the Bible verses about this and found that when the word *homosexual* was used in this context, it was accompanied by references to other transgressions such as sexual immorality, idolatry, adultery, prostitution, thievery, greed, drunkenness, slander, swindling, witchcraft, hatred, discord, jealousy, fits of rage, selfish ambition, dissension, factions, envy, orgies, obscenity, foolish talk, and course joking (1 Corinthians 6:9–10, Galatians 5:19, Ephesians 5:3–4). All of us have committed at least one of these sins, if not more, so if we take these verses literally, we are all going to hell. However, these verses do not mention hell. They say that people who engage in these behaviors will not inherit the kingdom of God.

There are different interpretations of the phrase *kingdom of God*. Some interpret it as meaning heaven, others as being a part

---

[2]   Fornication: Matthew 15:19; Mark 7:21; 1 Corinthians 5:1, 6:13, 18, and 7:2; 2 Corinthians 5:1; 1 Thessalonians 4:3; Jude 1:7.

[3]   Homosexuality: Leviticus 18:22, 20:13; Romans 1:32; 1 Corinthians 6:9; 1 Timothy 1:10.

of God's kingdom on earth (all those who choose to love and serve God), which is the way I interpret it. Once again, let us put the focus on the bigger picture rather than on individual sins. All of these behaviors are rooted in fear rather than in love. Fearful, selfish behaviors prevent us from fully participating in and enjoying the relationship God wants us to have with him and with each other in his kingdom on earth.

Loving others who are different from us and whom we've been conditioned to malign is easier if we understand a little bit about why they are the way they are. A few theories about why people identify as lesbian, gay, bisexual, or transgender follow.

1. *They are born this way.* Because these desires are not dominant in the majority of people and do not make as much biological sense as a heterosexual desire, this population is regarded as strange, different, or weird. When you consider everything that takes place in the nine months during which cells become a baby, it is amazing that any of us is born with everything working correctly. So many things can go wrong, and sometimes they do. Babies are born without limbs or organs, babies are born with mental impairments, babies are born as Siamese twins, and yes, I believe babies are sometimes born with their sexual or gender orientation wired differently. So why do we treat LGBT people differently? Why is growing up without a limb or an organ treated differently than growing up with a different sexual or gender orientation? Those with other physical or mental disabilities are given resources, surgeries, and other services to help them enjoy their lives even though they are considered different from normal people. When you talk with LGBT people, they will tell you they have felt different from a very young age, usually as early as preschool. Their orientation is not something they chose. Many will tell you they would love to be normal so they would not have to

endure the ridicule and discrimination they live with every day.

2. *They choose to be this way.* Often as people grow up and develop sexually they become confused about their sexuality. So they experiment, having both heterosexual and same-sex relationships, trying to determine if they are straight, bisexual, or homosexual. Some may use this as a way to rebel, showing their independence by defying what society considers normal.

3. *They were sexually abused growing up.* Childhood sexual abuse can mess with someone's understanding of what healthy sexuality is supposed to look and feel like. If you were a female who was repeatedly sexually abused by a male, as you grow up you may not feel sexually safe with a male and may gravitate toward a lesbian relationship. Boys who were sexually abused by men will sometimes grow up questioning their sexual orientation.

4. *Reincarnation.* For those who believe in reincarnation, this theory makes sense. If your spirit and your soul spent most of your past lives as a man having sexual relationships with women, your genetics are wired for you to be attracted to women. Now your spirit and your soul return to earth again, only this time in the body of a woman. But all your genetic programming from your past lives is geared toward female attraction, so chances are strong that in this lifetime you will be a lesbian.

5. *God created them this way on purpose, so there is nothing wrong with them, and they do not need to be transformed into heterosexual men and women.* This may be a difficult possibility for Christians to contemplate. While our sexuality should not define us, it is a core part of who we are. It is not

a sin, though what we do with our sexuality can sometimes lead to sin when used for selfish purposes regardless of our sexual orientation.

Is it possible for God to cure LGBT people? Can they become what is considered normal? Christians have created programs to cure them, and some homosexuals who have been through these programs say they are now heterosexual. But others who have participated were unable to change. Maybe those are the wrong questions. Is it possible for Christians to accept the LGBT community as fully normal and human, and if not, why not? I believe we are to love them just as they are, just as God loves and accepts each of us right where we are. Maybe we could develop relationships with them and get to know them for who they are rather than try to change them. Maybe we could thank God for them because they can teach us things about tolerance, diversity, and our own insecurities and judgmental attitudes. They were created by God just like the rest of us; we are all interconnected; we are all family in God's eyes.

"Our job on earth isn't to criticize, reject or judge. Our purpose it to offer a healing hand, compassion and mercy. We are to do unto others as we hope they will do unto us" (Dana Arcuri).

Chapter 3

Fear

All of us have encountered fear of one kind or another. Many books have been devoted entirely to this subject. In this chapter I will address what fear is, where fear comes from, how the church and Christians propagate fear, unhealthy and healthy fear, and how to replace fear with love.

Fear

Fear is the opposite of love; it produces distress and anxiety and immobilizes people. Love produces peace and joy and encourages people. I have found that most people are motivated more by fear than by love. God created each of us with dreams and abilities so we could enjoy our lives and bless those we come into relationship with. However, many people live mediocre lives, allowing fear to prevent them from pursuing their dreams and from becoming all that God created them to be.

A newborn baby has no fear. We are all born vibrating with pure love and trusting that our needs will be met. Fear is a learned response that we absorb when our parents and our environment fail to provide unconditional love and acceptance. Some babies will learn this right away if they are involved in a traumatic pregnancy or birth; or if their parents neglect their basic needs. Other babies will learn it at a later age.

Fear is instilled in people from a very young age in the American culture. Television shows and magazines are filled with everything that could cause us harm and that we need to fear and protect ourselves from. An isolated incident occurs, and they make it sound like it could happen to all of us now. Parents hover over their children, trying to protect them from any physical harm or emotional pain. Most of us were not taught how to identify, feel, and release fear, only how to internalize, medicate, run from, and avoid it.

The church and religion also promote fear. They talk about a God of love but raise fears concerning God's wrath and the consequences of sin. People experience fear if they do not attend church every week, if they do not contribute at least 10 percent of their gross income, if they disobey any of God's commandments, if they do not accept the official Jesus, or if they do not volunteer to help out in ministry outreaches. In this environment, many people are readier to fear God and to believe God is angry with them than they are to perceive God as love, to love him, and to receive his love.

I categorize fear into two types, unhealthy and healthy. Here are examples of unhealthy fear.

- *Fear of things that will most likely never happen.* You hear on the news that a plane has crashed and people have died, so now you refuse to fly on a plane even though more people are killed in car accidents than in plane crashes.

- *Fear of man's rejection.* Fear of man keeps you in bondage because you are never free to be the person God created you to be. You spend your days trying to impress people, trying to get them to love or to approve of you. Sometimes you deny yourself of wants or needs, or you let others take advantage of you to please them. You live as a slave to everyone around you, because you can never meet their unrealistic expectations of you.

- *Fear based on control.* This is how people, governments, religions, and employers attempt to motivate people. If you do not do what they ask or demand, something bad will happen to you or to your family. You comply because you fear the consequences, obeying out of resentment, anger, or frustration. If you try to instill fear to control others, you will get people to do what you want, but you will most likely damage relationships in the process.

- *Fear based on being raised in an environment where your needs were not met or you encountered abuse or neglect.* Your brain gets programmed to be on high alert at all times to protect yourself from people who could do or say things to cause you harm. You are motivated by fear, believing if you cannot find a way to control and to manipulate your environment and the people around you, your needs will never be met and you will not feel safe.

An example of healthy fear is a fear that protects you. Parents want their children to be fearful around fire so they do not burn themselves. A feeling of fear alerts you to danger around certain places or people so you can avoid them and protect yourself from possible harm. Another example is the fear of God, a respect, honor, and love for who God is rather than a fear that God will punish you if you do something wrong. Because God is love, fear cannot exist in him, so there is never any reason to be afraid of God.

For years I used fear to decide if I should do something. I reasoned that either the fear was there to keep me from doing something harmful or to immobilize me from doing something beneficial. Recently, the Holy Spirit informed me that I was not to use fear to make decisions, because I should be living from a place of love, not of fear. I was to use discernment, the ability to tune in to what the Holy Spirit was telling me. Spending time with God and learning how to hear his voice will increase your discernment abilities. Let us look at the example of public speaking. Many people have a fear of this that stems from being ridiculed or embarrassed when speaking in front of a class in school. Now as adults when approached about speaking in public they immediately feel fear and refuse to do it. A discernment response would be to first ask the Holy Spirit if they are supposed to speak and then to obey what the Spirit tells them to do.

In chapter 8 I discuss how God designed the human body and the world around us as an energy system. In this chapter I want to explain how to understand fear from this perspective. At its core everything is made up of vibrating energies. Fear is composed of low, dense vibrational frequencies. Love is the opposite, composed of high, light vibrational frequencies. You will always attract to yourself what you are giving out in terms of energy. If you are a loving person, it will be difficult for fear to attach itself to you, because the vibrational frequencies of love and fear are at opposite ends of the spectrum and thus cannot resonate with each other. If you tend to be a fearful person, you will attract fearful situations. That is why it is so important to release unhealthy fears rather than hang on to them. So how do you remove unhealthy fear and transform it into love? Here are some suggestions to get you started.

First, you need to become aware of how unhealthy fear manifests itself in your life. Ask the Holy Spirit to point this out to you so you can see your fear from God's perspective. Everything in your life stems from your thoughts and beliefs, so these are the first things that must change. What thoughts or beliefs are based on fear? Sometimes unhealthy fears are rooted in past trauma or abuse and are deeply ingrained in your subconscious mind. You may need the help of a good counselor to change this programming in your brain. Fortunately, some very good energy-based treatments can release these fears without forcing you to relive the past trauma.

Next, ask God to show you how to replace unhealthy fear-based thoughts and beliefs with love. How would you think, feel, or behave if you perceived a situation or a person from a place of love rather than of fear? People get used to living in fear. It becomes predictable and comfortable for them, and it is the way the majority of people live. Therefore, to release fear and to live from love can be scary at first. Jesus said that he came to set the captives free. We are all captives of fear but also have the ability to be set free from fear and to enter into a life of love.

Jesus lived in a world filled with fear but was able to live from love. He would spend time with his Father God, seeking advice and wisdom each day and getting daily downloads of love to dispense to the people he encountered. The next time you read the Gospels, make note of all the fear in the culture Jesus lived in, and also note how he responded from love rather than from fear to every situation he encountered. Jesus should be your example, and you have the ability to live from love just like he did, because you have access to the same heavenly Father and to the voice of the Holy Spirit that resides within you to guide you. The Bible teaches that perfect love casts out fear (1 John 4:18). God is perfect love (1 John 4:16), so the more you develop a relationship with God, the more love you will receive from him, driving out the fear in your life.

> *"There is no fear in love. But perfect love drives out fear, because fear has to do with punishment. The one who fears is not made perfect in love" (1 John 4:18).*

Chapter 4

Church Life

One of the things that surprised me on this spiritual journey was my discovery that much of what people believe and do in the church is based on fear. In this chapter I look at the contrast between the old law and the law of love, how sin is rooted in fear, how forgiveness takes us from a place of fear to love, the fears associated with church and with giving, and how the next great revival will be founded on love rather than on fear.

The Law Then and Now

When those of us who were brought up around church hear the word *law*, the first thing we usually think of is the Ten Commandments. We were taught that these were the most important laws for us to obey. I began looking at whom the Bible was speaking to when the Ten Commandments were written. There were primarily two types of people: Israelites and everyone else, including Egyptians and many others in groups with names ending in *ites*. They are sometimes referred to as aliens. The Israelites were the only group God seemed to address directly, doing so through chosen leaders like Moses. As you read through Exodus, Leviticus, and Deuteronomy, you see more and more laws added to the original Ten Commandments. These 613 laws are called the Torah. However, do you realize that these commandments and laws were given only to the Israelites? Therefore, if you, like me, are not Jewish, these laws do not directly apply to you.

So what was the purpose of all these laws? They were intended to remind the Israelites that they had a covenant relationship with God and that obedience to the law would bring them blessings and disobedience would bring them curses. I also believe the purpose may have been to show the Israelites that it was impossible for them to obey all the rules and to make the required sacrifices without a relationship with God. In the New Testament Jesus said that he fulfilled the old law through the new law of love: to love God, self, and others (Mark 12:30–31). The Bible teaches that this law of love is written on our consciousness or hearts (2 Corinthians 3:2–3) and that the Holy Spirit will instruct us how to live out this law (John 14:26).

So if people are not required to live under the old law, why do they continue to do so? Here are some possible reasons:

- People are not taught that the old law has been fulfilled by the new law.

- People have a difficult time believing God loves them just as they are and continue to feel the need to do something to earn God's love.
- People would rather have rules than relationships. Right and wrong, what to do, and what not to do have already been written out for them; all they have to do is read and obey the decrees. This does not require a relationship with God. Living the law of love, on the other hand, requires people to listen to the voice of the Holy Spirit to know what to do. This means they have to develop a relationship with the Holy Spirit so they can distinguish her voice from all the other voices in their heads.

Through parables and real-life stories, the Bible gives general knowledge about how to live and to treat people. The Holy Spirit then takes this general knowledge and makes it specific to each one of us. For example, the Bible tells us we are to work and not be lazy. The Spirit can tell you specifically what type of work you are to do and where you are to do it. The Bible tells us we are to be givers and to bless others with our resources. The Spirit will tell you whom to give to and how much to give. The Holy Spirit will never tell you to do something contrary to the law of love. For example, if you are tempted to harm someone, you know this is not the voice of the Spirit, so you should not do it.

This table shows the contrast between the old and the new law, demonstrating why the law of love is superior to the old law.

The Old Testament Law	The New Testament Law
What God required of the Israelites before Jesus came	What God required of everyone after Jesus came
People were required to perform rituals and sacrifices.	People are no longer required to perform rituals and sacrifices.

People were blessed when they obeyed God and cursed when they did not.	People are blessed by God because he loves them, not based on obedience.
People were sin-conscious, always thinking about what they were doing wrong.	People are love-conscious, always aware of how much God loves them.
People focused on serving God.	People focus on loving God.
People obeyed God from a place of fear to avoid punishment.	People obey God from a place of love.
People felt condemnation, with guilt and discouragement.	People feel conviction, with love and encouragement.

Anytime you revert back to living by the old law you are saying that what Jesus did and taught was not good enough and that you need to add your own effort. This is where grace comes in. God has done it all for you; there is nothing more you can do or need to do. Because of Jesus, all of God's riches are available to you: salvation, healing, finances, wisdom, deliverance, peace, love, and joy. All you have to do is believe and receive them.

> "'Allow me to explain the good news my religion proclaims,'
> said the preacher. The master was all attention. 'God is
> love. And God loves and rewards us forever if we observe
> God's commandments.' 'If?' said the master. 'Then the
> news isn't all that good, is it?'" (Anthony de Mello).

Sin

In church we are taught that we are sinners born with a sinful nature, that we are incapable of controlling our desires, that we need a savior to free us from sin, and that we cannot go to heaven if we commit certain sins. There is so much misinformation concerning sin that I asked the Holy Spirit to help rid me of all former beliefs about the subject so I could have a clearer understanding of what sin really is. Here is what I now believe.

There is only one sin, and that is the sin of ignorance. All other sins stem from this one. Before we came to planet Earth our spirits and our souls were with God in a perfect state of love. When we were born as human beings, a veil was placed over us so we could not remember where we had come from, making it easier to live on the planet. However, God planted within each of us a desire to reconnect with him, and we spend our lives looking for something or someone to fill this need for love. In the process we do a lot of things that harm ourselves and others. We call these things sins, and we usually refer to ourselves as sinners. Once we learn the truth about where we came from and are reconnected with God, we no longer live in ignorance. Now everything shifts and what we do is motivated by our love for God rather than our fear that God has abandoned us, or that he is going to punish us, or that we are all alone in the world.

God now sees us as the perfect, wonderful people he created us to be. We are now people who may choose to do something unloving, but that is not the same as being sinners. When we say, "I am a sinner," we are defining ourselves as sinners. When we say, "I committed a sin," we are reporting behavior that may be wrong but does not define who we are. We will become whatever we consistently believe and think about ourselves. If we continue to focus on being sinners, we will continue to struggle to overcome our sins. If we choose instead to focus on God's perception of who we are, this is who we will become. Our desire for sin will fade away as we become who God created us to be. I like the way Eckhart Tolle expressed this: "You do not become good by trying to be good, but by finding the goodness that is already within you, and allowing that goodness to emerge."[1]

When people attempt to define sin, they tend to concentrate on the big sins such as murder, adultery, drunkenness, abortion, divorce, sexual sins, greed, or lust. But sin can also mean being unkind, unloving, or unforgiving. Other people define sin as not obeying the Ten Commandments, missing the standard of behavior God has set forth. A definition I like is that sin is having a loveless perception.[2] We fail to perceive people and situations through the lens of God's love. I define sin as anything in my life that prevents me from having a loving relationship with God, self, or others.

Most sins are rooted in fear.

- You are afraid you will get in trouble, so you lie.
- You are afraid your need will not be met, so you steal.
- You are afraid you will not receive a good enough grade, so you cheat.
- You are afraid someone else will get the promotion, so you do something to make that person look bad.
- You are afraid of social situations, so you get drunk.
- You are afraid to feel, so you drink and take drugs.

I am sure you can add many more to this list. I do not believe that one sin is worse than any other since they all have the same result, separation from God and the people we have hurt. When we live under the law of grace, our love for God, for self, and for others motivates us to sin less and to love more. Many people mistakenly believe that sin is what sends them to hell. God does not send anyone to hell. People choose to go there, because they will have nothing to do with God, so they remain in ignorance, separated from him.

Many people believe that grace is permission to sin. We can do whatever we want because Jesus has already forgiven us. Grace is actually the opposite. It is the power not to sin. When our spirits are connected to the Holy Spirit, we have access to the supernatural empowerment needed to keep us from sin, and sin no longer controls us. The Bible teaches:

- "That we should no longer be slaves to sin" (Romans 6:6).
- "Count yourselves dead to sin but alive to God in Christ Jesus" (Romans 6:11).
- "For sin shall not be your master, because you are not under law, but under grace" (Romans 6:14).
- "No one who lives in him keeps on sinning" (1 John 3:6).
- "No one who is born of God will continue to sin, because God's seed remains in him; he cannot go on sinning, because he has been born of God" (1 John 3:9).

Does this mean we never sin? No, it means we have a choice rather than an obligation to sin. The Bible says, "Everything is permissible for me, but not everything is beneficial" (1 Corinthians 6:12). Therefore, while grace gives us permission to do all things, it is not always wise to do them. An easy example is cigarettes. They are legal to smoke but are not beneficial to our health. We can choose to do things that will harm ourselves and others, and God will continue to love us, but we may have to live with the negative consequences of our choices.

> *"We sinned for no reason but an incomprehensible lack of love, and he saved us for no reason but an incomprehensible excess of love" (Perter Kreeft).*

Forgiveness

The word *sin* is generally associated with repentance and forgiveness. I define repentance as admitting that you have committed some type of sin, learning from your mistake, and doing what you can to avoid committing this sin again. Due to the spiritual law of sowing and reaping, there will be a consequence for sin, but there will be no punishment. God has already forgiven you for every sin you will ever commit during your lifetime. Therefore, you do not have to keep asking for forgiveness every time you sin. Your responsibility is to repent and to receive God's forgiveness with a heart of gratitude.

The Bible teaches that because God has forgiven you, you are to forgive others. However, this is easier said than done. Forgiveness is a process that can take days or years to complete. Here are a few reasons you may delay forgiveness or choose not to forgive.

- You have a misunderstanding of what forgiveness is.
- You would have to release your anger, fear, or pride, traits that have become your identity and help protect you.
- You would have to relinquish your victim role, which keeps you from having to take responsibility for your life. It is much easier to blame your problems on other people or on what happened to you in the past.
- You would become vulnerable. By keeping up your defenses, you ensure no one will hurt you again. You forget that defenses also keep you from receiving love.
- You are waiting for the offender to ask for your forgiveness or to do something to prove deserving of it.

Here are some reasons you may want to forgive.
- God asks you to forgive, and since God created you, he knows what is best for you.
- Forgiveness transforms your thoughts and feelings from fear to love, bondage to freedom.

- Forgiveness is the ultimate preventive medicine and the greatest healer.
- When you allow yourself to remain wounded, bitter, or resentful, you contaminate not only yourself but everyone you come in contact with.
- Forgiveness releases you from the hold that another's attitudes and actions have over you.
- Forgiveness enables you to see the real person rather than the caricature you created after being hurt. You are able to see this person through God's eyes.

Just because you have forgiven someone does not mean you have to reconcile the relationship. Sometimes it is not safe to be around the person. Other times the person lives far away, is in prison, or has died. Sometimes the relationship can be partially restored. You may talk with or see a person once in a while, but this person does not have to be a major part of your life again. If it is safe and both people agree to it, a relationship can be fully restored after forgiveness. If you want to forgive those who have hurt you, here is some advice.

- It is not always wise to confront the person, especially if it is not safe for you. A person may become defensive or deny hurting you. Your healing does not depend on an admission of guilt or an apology from the offending person.
- Do not make excuses for those who have done you wrong. Denying or repressing what someone did to you only hurts you; internalized pain can leak out as emotional or physical illness. You need to be honest about what happened to you. Even Jesus expressed pain when he felt betrayed by others.
- Attempting to forget the event puts you in an unhealthy state of denial. Forgiveness is the ability to remember the event without the intense emotions associated with it.
- Do not wait for loving feelings; they usually come after you forgive, not before.

- Do not expect anything in return when you forgive. You are doing this for yourself, not for the other person.
- Forgiveness does not make the other person right, but it makes you free.

When you have wronged someone else, you may find yourself the most difficult person to forgive. If you still live under the law, you may beat yourself up with guilt and condemnation. You may replay what you did repeatedly in your mind. This is why it is so important to learn how to love yourself and to live under grace. Since God does not condemn you, neither should you.

There will be times when you may need to forgive God. We have all asked, "Why did he allow this?" or "If he is all-powerful, why did he not stop this?" or "If he loves me, why did he not protect me?" Many times you will not know the answers to these questions until you cross over to the other side. When you hold these unanswered questions against God, you will suffer. God will continue to love you, but you will build a wall of anger that prevents you from feeling his love. When you forgive God, the wall comes down and you can enjoy your relationship with him again. So how do you know when you have completely forgiven someone?

- You keep no record of wrongs. You do not keep bringing up what someone did to you in an attempt to hurt or to punish the person.
- You do not do or say things that would encourage the offender to be afraid of or to be intimidated by you.
- You no longer feel bitterness or desire vengeance that comes from deep resentment. You no longer need anger and hatred to protect yourself.
- You no longer identify yourself by past injuries and injustices. You are no longer a victim. The pain from your past no longer dictates how you live in the present nor does it determine your future.

- You desire that your offender forgive himself and have the same joy and freedom you now possess.
- You pray for God to bless the one who harmed you.
- You remain in a state of forgiveness toward the offender for the remainder of your lifetime.
- You enjoy your life again, filled with God's love, joy, and peace.

God is pure love, and we are to reflect God's character and to be his presence on earth. Jesus is the great example of how love lived out in human form appears. Jesus said that it is easy to love those who love us but that the challenge God sets before us is to learn to love our enemies. Forgiveness is one of the greatest forms of love. We all encounter people who hurt us, irritate us, or make our lives miserable. Instead of getting upset and angry at these people, see if you can find enough love with God's help to pray the following prayer.

"I bless you, dear friend, in all of your antagonistic ways. I bless you and I thank God for you and I forgive you and I release you. I let you go to your highest good. I thank you so much for the opportunity that you afforded me to forgive you with love." [4]

Church Revisited

I consider myself blessed to have been raised in a Christian home and to have participated in church from a young age. During my lifetime I have been a part of many denominations, including American and Southern Baptist, Presbyterian, Foursquare, Assembly of God, Pentecostal, Nazarene, and nondenominational. I have often been discouraged at how we separate ourselves from each other based on these belief systems. God considers all of us his children and part of the same family.

I believe each denomination exhibits a different part of who God is and what he desires. There is no way one church or denomination can offer everything related to Christianity and spirituality at one location. Each church and denomination specializes in something such as salvation, prophecy, spiritual gifts, healing, end-time theology, worship and music, service and good works, social justice, missions, helping the poor, or love and relationships. So when each church is doing what it is called to do, everything is getting done.

Here is an idea I would like to propose. Keep the current churches and denominations but allow Christians to choose one as a base camp. They would spend most of their time in this setting, making financial contributions, serving, and enjoying pastoral support. However, they would be free to move to another church anytime they felt led to do so without feeling guilty or hoping no one saw them there and told their pastor. For example, let's say my base church specializes in worship and music, but I love missions, so I go on a mission trip with another church in my city. If I want to learn about church history, I attend a weekly class on this topic at another church. Then at Thanksgiving, a different church has a great outreach to the poor, and I participate. In the process I develop friendships with my Christian brothers and sisters in different denominations. I also enjoy much more of the Christian life, learning and experiencing things that aren't available at my base church. Pastors should not be jealous of other churches and ministries but should encourage and bless each other, knowing we are all part of God's family.

There is nothing wrong with changing your base church if the Holy Spirit should lead you to do this. So many people remain with the same church or denomination their entire lives. The problem with this is that they get only a narrow understanding of what Christianity is all about since they receive the perspective of just one church, one pastor, or one denomination. Many times people stop growing spiritually but continue to attend because the family has belonged for generations and no one wants the guilt of being the first to leave the church. Others remain because they do not want to upset the pastor or because they fear what people will say about them. Once again they remain because they are living in fear. I am not suggesting that you move to another church every five years, but I am encouraging you to ask the Holy Spirit every so often if this is where you are to remain or if there is a different church for you. Seek your heart to find the real motivation for being at a particular church.

So what about choosing not to attend church? The Bible says, "Let us not give up meeting together, as some are in the habit of doing" (Hebrews 10:25), and we immediately interpret this to mean church. Nowhere does this verse mention the word *church.* Cannot this verse also pertain to having lunch with a friend, spending time with your family, attending a concert or other social event, or working on a service project? Since the Holy Spirit lives within us, we take her wherever we go. We live in an interactive age and can receive spiritual truth through books, sermons, online teachings and churches, Christian events, radio and television shows, and many other options in addition to a Sunday morning service. People are concerned about declining church attendance in America. Maybe instead of counting how many people show up on Sunday morning, we should start counting how many people in our community experience God's love each week.

One of the things I find fascinating about Jesus was his response to the traditional religious hierarchy that was in place when he lived.

He did not want to be a part of it other than occasionally speaking in the temple, and he exposed its leaders' hypocrisy. At no time did he ask for or encourage people to turn his life and his teachings into a religion or to have people worship him. Jesus always pointed people to God as the source of everything and as the One who should be worshiped. So why or how is it that we have ignored this and have created the very religious structures Jesus opposed? Every religion, including Christianity, has an organized structure, power, wealth, and rules. Is our dependence on Jesus and the Holy Spirit or is it on a church institution or a set of doctrines?

Jesus did not leave us with a religious system; he left us with a relationship. There are many ways to express and to experience this relationship. Church should be about how we live and express love to others. It shouldn't be about showing up in a building with the same group of people every week and then putting guilt on those who choose not to appear on a particular Sunday—or praising those who attend every service as if this makes them closer to God or more righteous. God's love for us is the same whether or not we attend church.

A good way to check your motivation for going to church is to skip one Sunday and then see how you feel and what thoughts go through your head. If you are living under the law you may feel guilt for not going, or you may think there is something wrong with you for not feeling guilt. You may find yourself worrying about what others will say or think about you. When your heart is in the right place, you should be able to enjoy your day guilt-free and feel God's presence even when you are not in church on a Sunday. Am I writing this to encourage everyone to quit attending church? No, I enjoy church and will continue to be a part of church life. However, I think it is important that we be honest with ourselves about why we attend and that we give grace and love to those who choose other ways to express their relationship with God, even when it is outside of a church building.

Spirit-Led Giving

There are many ways we can give when serving in church. We can give of our time, our talents, and our financial resources. I find it interesting that while many churches say they operate under grace rather than the law, they have a difficult time giving up the law of tithing. They love to cite Malachi 3:6–12. Essentially God is saying that if people consistently gave their tithe to him, their lives would be blessed. I do not disagree with this concept, but under grace we are told "each man should give what he has decided in his heart to give, not reluctantly or under compulsion; for God loves a cheerful giver" (2 Corinthians 9:7). So there may be times when you give more than 10 percent of your income and times when you give less. Either way you should feel no guilt if you are obeying the Holy Spirit. When you listen to the Spirit you will know when, how much, and where to give; there is no reason to worry whether you should tithe on your gross or your net income. Some people get upset when churches ask for money, but a church is a business with expenses that need to be paid for each month. Therefore, if you enjoy the church you attend, bless and support it through your giving.

Giving is more about our attitude than about the amount we give. Years ago when I first started giving money to a church, I did not have a good attitude. I saw so many personal needs that the money could meet. I was giving from a place of fear, guilt, and obligation rather than of love. So one day God told me to put only a dollar in the offering plate every time it was passed until I could do it with a good attitude; then I could give more. Another time, after I had tithed consistently for years, God told me to stop and not to give any money to the church for at least a month. Apparently I needed another attitude adjustment. The thoughts in my head were:

- What will people think when they see I never put anything in the offering plate?

- What will the people who keep track of who gives what think about me when they see I quit giving?
- If I quit giving, something bad will happen to me.

Yes, once again without my realizing it, I was giving from a place of fear, law, and people pleasing rather than from a place of love for God.

Everything we have is a gift from God to enjoy and to share with others. Nothing is ours to keep. When we live from this perspective it is easier to share and to give to others. Money is just a tool for us to use to meet our needs and to bless others. I have often heard people say that it's better to buy a house because renting is just throwing money away. I prefer to look at renting as a way to bless someone each month with the rent check. Many of us were raised to look for the cheapest price when shopping so we could save money. While there is nothing wrong with this, sometimes it is worth paying more to bless a person or a business. God is generous, and we can represent him better when we are generous with the blessing he has given us.

Besides providing money, we can give in our service to others. I believe the only reason we should volunteer to serve at church or in a ministry is because we have prayed about it and the Holy Spirit has told us to do it. Many people feel burned out or have quit going to church because their motivation for serving was wrong. They served:

- Out of need.
- Out of guilt.
- To please someone.
- To get someone to notice them.
- Because they feared what people would think of them if they did not serve.
- Because of peer pressure.

Sometimes people continue to serve long after the Spirit wants them to, because they believe that if they quit, no one will take their place or that after all the hard work they have invested in a ministry, it could fall apart when they leave. If the ministry is to continue, the Holy Spirit will speak to someone to come forward and continue it. Some church ministries are perpetual and must continue year after year, while others are needed for a specific time period after which their purpose comes to an end. We need to know how to discern the difference.

So whether you offer money, time, or service, rather than give from a place of fear, give from a place of love as the Spirit leads you.

"A pessimist, they say, sees a glass as being half empty; an optimist sees the same glass as half full. But a giving person sees a glass of water and starts looking for someone who might be thirsty." (G. Donald Gale)

The Next Great Revival

Throughout church history there have been many times and styles of revival. We usually define a revival as a religious service held to awaken people to something they have not heard before or to restore them to something they previously believed. Today, many prophetic people are talking and writing about the coming "last day's revival." It is expected to usher the greatest number of people into the kingdom of God. Believers say we will see miraculous things because God's power and presence will be so strong. They predict this revival will come not from the top down but from everyday people who are not popular or known at this time. These people have been hidden, being prepared by God for this revival. They will emphasize salvation, deliverance, and healing.

While I believe all the above to be true, I am troubled that we are looking to past revivals and expecting God to do the same thing, only on a grander scale, rather than expecting God to do something we have never witnessed before. The focus is on how God will change nonbelievers but not us. Sometimes I wonder if Christians will recognize this next great move of God since it may be so different from what they are expecting. These are things I pray will be part of that great move.

- We are transformed by the Holy Spirit to be people motivated by love rather than by fear.
- We no longer live under the law of judgment, fear, lack, close-mindedness, sin, sickness, guilt, and condemnation in our churches, in our lives, and in the way we treat others.
- We realize that what makes us Christian is simply that we believe who Jesus said he was and choose to live our lives by his teachings. It is not church doctrine, membership, or statements of belief that make us Christians.
- We allow God to manifest himself differently through each of us instead of insisting Christians all look and act alike. We realize we are all on our own spiritual journeys and respect

our differences as we learn and grow from and with each other.

- We realize there is much we can learn from those who do not consider themselves Christians or who are of a different religious affiliation.
- We realize all humans were created by God even if they have not yet found him. Therefore, we will treat them with love and respect rather than as projects we need to convert.
- We realize how interconnected we are with each other, with nature, with animals, with the spiritual realm, and with everything around us—the things we can and cannot see with our eyes.
- We realize that the development of our spirits and our souls is far more important than meeting all the desires of our bodies. As Pierre Teilhard de Chardin wrote, "We are not human beings having a spiritual experience. We are spiritual beings having a human experience."

Jesus said they will know us by our love. May genuine love for God, ourselves, and others be the driving force in this next great revival.

Chapter 5

Jesus

I believe Jesus to be one of the most controversial figures ever to live on planet Earth. I was raised to believe certain things about Jesus and never questioned them. However, while on this spiritual journey I decided to get rid of everything I had been taught, to look at Jesus as if I knew nothing about him, and to read what people outside of the Christian faith had to say about him. In this chapter I write about who Jesus is to me, where Jesus was during the missing years, the Aramaic language Jesus spoke, the teachings of Jesus, alternative ways to interpret salvation, and why Jesus died.

Jesus

Sometimes it is difficult to know what to do with Jesus. Some people believe:

- He is just another spiritual teacher or prophet sent from God.
- He came to show us the way to heaven when we die.
- He came to die on a cross in our place for our sins.
- We are to have a relationship with him.
- We are to worship him.
- We are to tell everyone about him.
- Everyone will eventually find Jesus on his or her own.

Is it possible to define who Jesus was? The Christian church has a nice box it likes to put Jesus in, but I no longer believe we can keep him in a box just as we could not keep him in the grave. I like what psychotherapist Thomas Moore said: "Jesus was not showing us how to live life as much as he was showing us how to allow life to be lived through us."[1] Jesus was able to live a fully human life. He enjoyed being with friends, eating, laughing, cooking, walking, sharing, talking, traveling, and spending time alone. Jesus was also able to live a full life as a spiritual being. He spent time with his Father God through prayer, had supernatural experiences, and taught and lived out spiritual truths. He lived simultaneously in the physical and the spiritual realms. I believe Christians have spent too much time focused on the death and resurrection of Jesus and not enough on his life. These aspects of him must be placed in balance; one is not more important than the other.

When Jesus looks down on the earth and sees what we have done with his life, his teaching, and his death, is he pleased or does he wonder how we could have misinterpreted the things he stood for? I do not believe he came so we could create a religion and a theology and then try to convert as many people as possible, using fear tactics. Humans have a tendency to want to control ideas and people and to make everyone think and believe the same things. Jesus encouraged people to ponder his teachings rather than tell them how or what to think, believe, or feel. And while he talked about the church, I think he was referring to people who follow his teachings and not to the big religious business organization it has become. Here is what I believe about Jesus.

- He was the essence of who God is in human form, the Son of God, a part of the Trinity, around since the beginning of all creation.
- He came to live among us to show us who God is—a loving God, not the angry, vengeful God portrayed in the Old Testament.
- He came to show us what love looks like in action and how to treat ourselves and others.
- He came to show us we are both physical and spiritual beings and how to live connected to both facets of ourselves simultaneously.
- He came to show us that death is nothing to fear, that it is just a transition of our spirits and our souls from the earthly world to the spiritual realm.
- He died because he was teaching things that challenged the political and religious leaders of the day, and they feared that there would be an uprising, that they would lose control of the people, and that Jesus would become a king and take over.
- He came to show us our ignorance, the illusions we accept, and the lies we believe about life and the spiritual realm.
- He was a rebel who courageously spoke truth and lived outside the expectations and rules of the society he lived in at that time.
- He came to show us the way, and then he returned to God. However, he left the Holy Spirit in his place. So it is the Holy Spirit, not Jesus, whom we are to have a relationship with, follow, depend on, and abide in.

I believe Jesus came to earth to reconnect us to his Father God and to teach us everything we need to know to become love so we can transform the earth into a more loving and peaceful place connected to the spiritual realm in, around, and above us. I realize we are not usually taught this in church; many of us were taught that the only reason Jesus came to earth was to die on a cross to win forgiveness of our sins so we can go to heaven when we die. I now see this as a very limiting belief. The more I study the life and the teachings of Jesus the more expansive his earthly mission becomes to me and the more thankful I am to be his follower.

"The Jews tried to keep Christ contained within their law, while the Greeks tried to turn Him into a philosophy; the Romans made of Him an empire; the Europeans reduced Him to a culture, and we Americans have made a business of Him" (Unknown).

Where Was Jesus during the Missing Years?

When we think about the life of Jesus we focus on his birth and then jump into his ministry thirty years later. So where was Jesus from ages thirteen to thirty? I had always been told that if it was important for us to know that it would have been in the Bible. But having learned that the Bible is just one of many sources for spiritual understanding, I wanted to find the answer to this question. Anyone over thirty knows how your teens and your twenties affect who you are as a person and what you believe. So wherever Jesus was and whatever he was doing had to have had a big impact on his spiritual perspective on life.

I found a variety of sources that attempted to answer this question. They all agreed that he left at thirteen because that was the age when parents found a wife for their son, and he had no desire to get married. Some sources said Jesus spent those years traveling around the Middle East and Asia Minor, doing carpentry work to earn a living and engaging in conversations with people from spiritual traditions other than his own Jewish heritage. Other sources said he traveled to Nepal and India with one of the many trading caravans that would travel this route. Initially I thought this was a crazy idea. However, when I started looking into it, I found documented evidence that this theory could be true.

The earliest documentation I could find was from 1887 when Russian journalist Nicolas Notovitch traveled to Tibet and India to learn about the people and their customs. He discovered that there was a Buddhist monastery where ancient memoirs about Jesus Christ were kept. (In the language of this area at that time people referred to Jesus Christ as Issa.) He was given permission to read them and to write down the information. Later, he published this account but was unable to get anyone to promote it, because the information in the manuscripts would have caused too much controversy in the Christian religions.[2] In his book *The Unknown Life of Jesus Christ,* Notovitch translated the ancient memoirs about Jesus into English. These memoirs discuss the birth of Jesus, his departure from his father's house to avoid marriage, and what he did during his years away. The manuscripts also mention Moses, the plague in Egypt, and the exodus. They say that the Buddhist monks revered Issa as one of the greatest spiritual teachers of all time. Here are some interesting things I found in these memoirs about Jesus.[3]

- The priests of Brahma "taught him to read and to understand the Vedas, to cure physical ills by means of prayers, to teach and to expound the sacred scriptures, to drive out evil desires from man and make him again in the likeness of God."[4]
- "Issa taught to 'Pray not to idols, for they cannot hear you; hearken not to the Vedas where the truth is altered; be humble and humiliate not your fellow-man.'"[5]
- The life of Issa was threatened because he opposed the idols, gods, and goddesses and the way the powerful treated the poor.[6]
- "The earth trembled and the heavens wept, because of the great crime committed in the land of Israel. For there was tortured and murdered the great and just Issa, in whom was manifest the soul of the Universe. Which had incarnated in a simple mortal, to benefit men and destroy the evil spirit in them; to lead back to peace, love and happiness, man, degraded by his sins, and recall him to the one and indivisible Creator whose mercy is infinite."[7]

In 1922, Swami Abhedananda went to India to study Buddhism and to visit the Himis monastery to determine if Notovitch had been there and had seen the manuscripts about Jesus. The monks confirmed this to be true, and Swami Abhedananda, like Notovitch, was given access to these manuscripts.[8] He also published an account about his journey and what he read in the manuscripts titled *Kasmir O Tibbate (In Kasmir and Tibet)*. Here are excerpts of what he found in the manuscripts.

- "The Lord of the Universe blessed this firstborn child to reward their patience and sent him to save the sinners and cure the afflicted. This divine child was named Issa. During his childhood he exhorted people to be devoted and respectful to the one Lord of the Universe and sinners to abstain from sinful acts and to repent. People from everywhere came to listen to the wise sayings from the mouth of this child, and the sons of Israel unanimously proclaimed that the infinite, merciful Supreme Soul who knows no beginning, no end, existed in this child."[9]
- "Issa was unwilling to marry. He had already attained fame by his expositions of the nature of God. At the proposal of marriage, he decided to leave his father's house in secret."[10]
- "He left Jerusalem, joined a group of traders, and set out for the land of Sind (the lower Indus valley, South Pakistan) where they used to purchase merchandise for export to various countries."[11]
- "Thus he returned to his homeland at the age of twenty-nine and began spreading the word of peace amongst his oppressed countrymen."[12]

In 1924, Nicholas Roerich, an archaeologist, anthropologist, explorer, hunter, diplomat, mystic, poet, author, lecturer, and artist, led an expedition through Central Asia in his quest for truth.[13] Along the way he passed through the monastery in Himis where he also found evidence of the Issa manuscripts. During his travels he spoke with many of the uneducated common people, who told him stories about seeing and hearing Issa teach.[14] In 1925, Roerich wrote about his travels and about what he found in the manuscripts. Here are some excerpts.

- Issa spoke out against the religious leaders, saying, "Worship not the idols. Do not consider yourself first. Do not humiliate your neighbor. Help the poor. Sustain the feeble. Do evil to no one. Do not covet that which you do not possess, but which is possessed by others."[15]

- The religious leaders did not like this and decided to kill Issa. "But Issa, forewarned by the Sudras, departed from this place by night."[16]

- "Issa taught that men should not strive to behold the Eternal Spirit with one's own eyes but to feel Him with the heart, and to become a pure and worthy soul."[17]

- Jesus was "joyously accepted by monks and people of the lower class. And Jesus taught in the monasteries and in the bazaars, wherever the simple people gathered, there he preached."[18]

- "Not far from this place lived a woman whose son had died and she brought him to Jesus. And in the presence of a multitude, Jesus laid his hand on the child, and the child rose healed. And many brought their children and Jesus laid his hands upon them, healing them."[19]

- "Jesus said to them, 'I came to show human possibilities. What has been created by me, all men can create. And that which I am, all men will be. These gifts belong to all nations and all lands, for this is the bread and water of life.'"[20]

In 1939, Elizabeth Caspari, a Swiss music professor, went on a pilgrimage to Tibet and was also shown these manuscripts about Jesus.[21] She was not interested in writing anything down but was profoundly affected by what she read and wondered "if what John wrote in his book, about the many other things that Jesus did that the whole world would not have room enough to record them, was referring to the time Jesus spent in Asia."[22]

What I found fascinating about what Jesus was doing from thirteen to thirty was how his life in Tibet and India paralleled his life in Israel. He taught similar things, healed the sick, and spoke out against the religious authorities who kept people under the bondage of laws and who wanted to kill him. I also found it interesting that it was through the Eastern religions, which I had always been taught are in opposition to Christianity, that Jesus learned how to teach, to heal, and to drive out demons. After researching this, I believe that Issa and Jesus were indeed the same man.

> *"And Jesus grew in wisdom and stature and in*
> *favor with God and men" (Luke 2:52).*

The Aramaic Language

To understand who Jesus is and the meaning behind the words he spoke and the stories he told, it is important to know about the culture in which Jesus lived. One day the Holy Spirit asked me about this culture, and I realized how little I knew. The Spirit reminded me that it was a Middle Eastern culture based on traditions alien to our Western mind-set. Many of the people who translated the Bible and decided what books to include in it were from the European culture. I never realized what a problem that was until I started reading about the culture of the Aramaic people, whose language Jesus spoke.

One of the interesting things I learned is that in the Aramaic language there is meaning not just in the written word but in the sound, in how a word is spoken aloud. Unfortunately, this meaning gets lost in written form. I discovered that due to our Western mind-set we have misinterpreted parts of Jesus's teaching and have lost some of their intended meaning. One of the books that helped me to understand this is *Let There Be Light* by Rocco Errico.[23] He writes about understanding the words and the life of Jesus through the idioms, mysticism, culture, and amplification of the Aramaic language.

Idiom is a figure of speech that says one thing but means something else, such as the phrase "raining cats and dogs." The Bible contains more than a thousand idioms that were translated literally and not identified for what they were. Genesis 19:26 says Lot's wife "looked back and she became a pillar of salt." This is an idiom meaning that she suffered a stroke, became paralyzed, and died. Jesus told his followers that "they will pick up snakes with their hands; and when they drink deadly poison, it will not hurt them" (Mark 16:18). "Will pick up snakes" means they will handle fearlessly the challengers and enemies of his gospel. "Drink deadly poison" means the power to overcome all malicious gossip and false accusations made against his disciples. Paul's "thorn in my flesh" (2 Corinthians 12:7) means a troublemaker.

Mysticism is the pursuit of knowledge through subjective, intuitive experience. Forty percent of the Bible is based on dreams, visions, and revelations. When you see the phrase *to appear* in the Bible it often means to come by revelation in a vision or a dream rather than a literal appearance. I found it interesting that in the book of Acts the church was guided more by intuition, dreams, and spiritual revelation than by boards or committees.

The culture of the Middle East also helps us understand the Bible. "A baby is swaddled" (Luke 2:7) is symbolic testimony that the parents will raise the child to be truthful and faithful. Jesus told his disciples to "travel without carrying purse, script or shoes" (Matthew 10:9–10) because carrying extra shoes or clothing would invite robbers to attack them, and Jesus wanted them to be able to travel without fear. "Do this in remembrance of me" (Luke 22:19) means "I love you; therefore, I am always with you."

Amplification is similar to what we would call exaggeration. In conversation people in the Middle East want to convey an impression by any suitable means rather than deliver a message in accurate, detailed terms like people in Western cultures. People in the Middle Eastern culture like to speak in pictures and figurative language. When Jesus used the words "truly, truly" (Mark 14:9) he was letting us know there was no amplification in what he was about to say. An example of amplification is the report that Samson "killed a thousand soldiers with the jawbone of an ass" (Judges 15:15–16). Abraham's descendants were to be "as the sand of the seashore" (Genesis 13:16).

Here are some Bible verses followed by their meaning in the Aramaic language.

Bible Verse	Aramaic Meaning
We are told that when Jesus was on the cross he said, "My God, my God, why have you forsaken me?" (Matthew 27:46).	It has never made sense to me how God could forsake himself or why a God of love would forsake his Son. But in the Aramaic language this means "O Sustainer, O Sustainer, to what a purpose you have left me to fulfill a destiny."[24]
"God is a righteous judge, a God who expresses his wrath every day" (Psalm 7:11).	"God is a just judge and he is not angry every day."[25]
"Be still and know that I am God" (Psalm 46:10).	"Return to me and know that I am God!" [26]
"Blessed are the poor in spirit, for theirs is the kingdom of heaven" (Matthew 5:3).	"Delighted are those who surrender to God, for theirs is the kingdom of heaven."[27]
"I am the light of the world" (John 8:12).	"My teaching enlightens the world of humanity."[28]

I found it interesting that while I have been in church all of my life and had heard about the Greek and the Hebrew versions, I had never heard anything about the Aramaic language that Jesus spoke and how it changes the interpretation of his words.

Every individual is at once the beneficiary and the victim of the linguistic tradition into which he has been born" (Aldous Huxley).

The Teachings of Jesus

Teachings were at the heart of Jesus's ministry and continue to influence people today. He lived at a time when books were rare and literacy low, so knowledge was passed down through oral teachings. We can understand the teachings of Jesus on two levels: the natural physical interpretation and the spiritual interpretation. Most of the time Jesus was teaching on both levels simultaneously, but only those with ears to hear were able to receive the deeper spiritual meaning. People interpret the teachings of Jesus based on their own world views, life experiences, and religious upbringings. I had always understood his teachings from the Christian context I had been taught but have now discovered there are many other meanings behind his words. Here are alternative ways to interpret some of his teachings.

Traditional Interpretation	Alternative Interpretation
Jesus said, "I am the way, and the truth, and the life. No one comes to the Father except through me" (John 14:6). The traditional interpretation is that no one can come to God, heaven, or eternal life except through belief in what Jesus did on the cross.	Could this also be interpreted as meaning that no one comes to the knowledge of the Father God except through the teaching of Jesus, which is love?

"The kingdom of God is within you" (Luke 17:21) is usually interpreted as meaning that when we accept Jesus he lives inside of us as the Holy Spirit.	Could this also be interpreted as meaning that everything God is and everything we need from him have already been deposited within our spirits? We do not have to look outside ourselves; we need to look inward through prayer, meditation, and contemplation to find truth, peace, and love.
At the wedding feast, Jesus changed the water into wine, and we identify this event as the first miracle he performed, focusing on the fact that he saved the best for last.	Could this also mean that "the water represented living an ordinary life and the wine represented living a life that is spiritually alive"?[29]
When we eat the communion bread and drink the wine, we are aware of the traditional teaching that the bread represents Jesus's body on the cross and the wine represents the blood he shed there, and we reflect on Jesus dying for our sins.	Could this also mean that "as you chew the bread and drink the wine you are spiritually being transformed, becoming transparent, translucent, spiritually alive, visionary and profoundly communal with those around you"?[30] Another interpretation is that the bread represents our physical life and the wine our spiritual life and that when we take communion we realize the unity of the physical and spiritual parts of our existence.

79

"You hypocrite, first take the plank out of your own eye, and then you will see clearly to remove the speck from your brother's eye" (Matthew 7:5). The traditional teaching is that this means we must deal with our own faults before pointing them out in others.	Could the plank refer to interpreting the words of Jesus through the dark lens of an old religious belief system? When we remove it, might we be able to see clearly enough to understand the deeper spiritual meaning behind Jesus's teachings?
Jesus referred to God as Father because he was born without a biological father.	Could Jesus have called God his Father to indicate a deity more loving and caring than the often-aloof Yahweh of the Old Testament?[31]
Jesus teaches us to "enter through the narrow gate. For wide is the gate and broad is the road that leads to destruction, and many enter through it" (Matthew 7:13). The traditional interpretation is that the narrow gate refers to accepting Jesus and going to heaven, and the wide gate means rejecting Jesus and going to hell. But nothing in the context of this verse indicates it has to do with how we get to heaven or hell.	Could the narrow gate refer to living a life motivated by love and the wide gate refer to living a life motivated by fear?

"For God so loved the world that he gave his one and only son that whoever believes in him shall not perish but have eternal life. For God did not send his Son into the world to condemn the world, but to save the world through him" (John 3:16–17). The traditional interpretation is that "he gave" refers to Jesus's death on the cross, and "believes in him" means believing in what Jesus did on the cross.	Could this be interpreted another way? "For God so loved the world that he gave his only son to come live among us, that whoever believes in his teachings should not die but have everlasting life. For God did not send his Son into the world to condemn the world but that the world through his teachings and life example could be saved from ignorance and fear and learn to live from love."

We are trained to believe there is only one right way to understand the teachings of Jesus, so we do not allow ourselves to ponder any other interpretations. This reluctance is based on fear of how God or other Christians will view us if we do not get it right or agree with the majority view. One of the things I enjoy about the Holy Spirit is her willingness to share other perspectives when we are open to listen and to consider them. Whether we interpret the teachings of Jesus correctly or not, God's love for us remains the same.

"The mediocre teacher tells, the good teacher explains, the superior teacher demonstrates and the great teacher inspires" (William Arthur Ward).

Salvation

If there is one word associated with Jesus more than any other in the church it may be *salvation*. The standard teaching is that people are born sinners and need to be saved through Jesus's death and resurrection so they can be forgiven and go to heaven when they die; they are saved when they receive Jesus as their Lord and Savior. In the church we often hear certain terms associated with this concept of salvation including *to save your soul, to be born again, to accept Christ, to repent,* and *Jesus cleanses me.* I had never questioned the meaning of salvation until the Holy Spirit showed me other ways to understand these phrases. Here are some interesting interpretations.

The Phrase	The Alternative Meaning
To repent and to believe the gospel	"He was not asking them to be sorry for their sins and embrace an orthodox theology. He was asking them to forfeit their own agenda and embrace his. It is not whether we want to go to heaven or hell, but whether we want to trust God or continue trusting ourselves."[32]
Jesus cleanses us.	"He completely removes all loveless thoughts. We relinquish any thoughts of judgment that hold us to the past. We relinquish any thoughts of attachment that keep us grasping at the future."[33]
To save your soul	"To cleanse your soul of negative memories, of misconceptions, of things that are not your natural right and to allow there to be a constant inflow from the spirit of you which brings you joy, prosperity and good health."[34]

To accept Christ	"I accept the beauty within me as who I really am. I am not my weakness. I am not my anger. I am not my small-mindedness. I am much, much more. And I am willing to be reminded of who I really am."[35]
To be born again	"Letting go of a story, the story of not being worthy enough, not being loved, not being one with the God within you."[36]

I like these interpretations of salvation. In the past I defined salvation as a one-time event when someone received Jesus as Lord and Savior. However, I no longer understand salvation as just this onetime event, but as a lifetime of inner transformation that continues long after this one-time event as our heart, led by the Holy Spirit, continues to release anything in us that is not love so that we can become more like Jesus.

"The reality of loving God is loving him like he's a Superhero who actually saved you from stuff rather than a Santa Claus who merely gave you some stuff" (Criss Jami).

Why Jesus Died

You may be wondering why I would write about this topic as the answer seems so obvious to those of us raised in a church setting. And I realize by questioning this I am stepping into territory I probably should not venture into since I am not a theologian. However, I found this topic fascinating to consider and to explore. I had always been told and had believed that Jesus died to forgive us of our sins so we could go to heaven when we die. However, during this spiritual journey the Holy Spirit asked me if Jesus ever mentioned the purpose of his death. I realized that many of the New Testament writers had their own thoughts on why Jesus died, but I wanted to know what Jesus himself had to say on this subject. So I read all the words of Jesus in the red-letter edition of my Bible and was surprised to discover that he talked a lot about his purpose in coming to earth but talked very little about the reason for his death. He said that he knew he would be dying, that he would be betrayed, that he would suffer a painful death, and that he would rise again. These were the messages he repeatedly gave his disciples. The only passages I could find where Jesus may have hinted at why he had to die were:

- "I know you are Abraham's descendants, yet you are ready to kill me, because you have *no room for my word*" (John 8:37).
- "But Jesus said to them, *I have shown you many great miracles from the Father.* For which of these do you stone me?" (John 10:32).
- "For even the Son of Man did not come to be served but to serve and to *give his life as a ransom for many*" (Mark 10:45). Could this mean that he came to earth to show us through his life how to live from love so we could be ransomed from fear-based lives?
- "The Christ will suffer and rise from the dead on the third day, *and repentance and forgiveness of sins will be preached*

in his name to all nations" (Luke 24:46–47). Could this be interpreted as meaning that after he died and rose again, people would finally understand what he had been teaching them when he was alive, the message of repentance and forgiveness? (Jesus was already forgiving people before he died, so his death on the cross was not necessary for repentance and forgiveness.)

- "This is my blood of the covenant, which is poured out for many for *the forgiveness of sins*" (Matthew 26:28). Here again, Jesus was already forgiving people before he died, so his death was not necessary for the forgiveness of sins. The Jesus Seminar says its research shows that these are not the words of Jesus, that the disciples took his ideas and put them in their own words.[37]

- "Just as the Father knows me, and I know the Father and I lay down my *life for the sheep*" (John 10:15). "No one takes it from me, but I lay it down of my own accord. I have authority to lay it down and I have authority to take it again" (John 10:18). Jesus lets us know he has the authority to choose when he dies, but he still does not tell us why he would die other than for the sheep, which are generally thought to mean the people who follow him.

In addition to emphasizing his death on a cross, the church focuses on the fact that Jesus rose from the dead. The church says this is important because it shows that we will all rise from the dead to new life in heaven. The resurrection shows the power that God has to do miraculous things. It proves the accuracy of Old Testament prophecies. It shows that Satan was unable to keep Jesus dead in the ground. However, we talk about Jesus's resurrection as if he were the only one ever to have done this. When you read the Bible you find people both before and after Jesus who were dead and were resurrected back to life.

1. Elijah raised the son of the Zarephath widow from the dead (1 Kings 17:19–22).

2. Elisha raised the son of the Shunammite woman from the dead (2 Kings 4:32–5).
3. A man was raised from the dead when his body touched Elisha's bones (2 Kings 13:20–21).
4. Many people rose from the dead at the resurrection of Jesus (Matthew 27:52–53).
5. Jesus raised the son of the widow of Nain from the dead (Luke 7:12–15).
6. Jesus raised the daughter of Jairus from the dead (Luke 8:49–55).
7. Jesus raised Lazarus from the dead (John 11:38–44).
8. Peter raised Dorcas from the dead (Acts 9:40–41).
9. Paul raised Eutychus from the dead (Acts 20:9–12).

All of these resurrections prove that there is life after death, that God has the power to do miraculous things, and that Satan does not have the power to keep people dead whom God wants alive. The only thing I can find that differentiates Jesus's resurrection from these other resurrections is that he fulfilled the prophecies about his death.

Jesus is also known for ascending to heaven while still living. I was always fascinated with his ascension but rarely heard a sermon about this event or a discussion of its significance. Apparently it signified the end of Jesus's work on earth, his return to his Father in heaven, and the fact that Jesus was now glorified and no longer in his human state. However, he was not the only person in the Bible to ascend rather than to die a normal human death.

1. "Enoch walked with God; then he was no more, because God took him away" (Genesis 5:24).
2. "As they were walking along and talking together, suddenly a chariot of fire and horses of fire appeared and separated the two of them, and Elijah went up to heaven in a whirlwind" (2 Kings 2:11).

3. "By faith Enoch was taken from this life, so that he did not experience death; he could not be found, because God had taken him away" (Hebrews 11:5).

So the three things we associate with Jesus's death—crucifixion, resurrection, and ascension—were not unique to Jesus since people before and after him had experienced them.

While Jesus never clearly discussed the reason he had to die, he did talk a lot about the purpose of his life and what he wanted to teach people while he was here. But he never said he had to die in order for people to receive everything he was teaching. He said we had to believe in his teachings and to accept that he was who he said he was, God's Son. I believe he died because he was preaching a message that political and religious leaders saw as a threat. They thought the only way to stop Jesus from preaching his message of love was to kill him. Based on his words there appears to be no other reason for Jesus's death. It was only after he was gone that people felt the need to connect his life teachings to his death to explain why he had died.

Through the teachings of Jesus, not his death, we learned about our separation from God and our need to repent, to forgive, and to live from love rather than from fear. We also learned that we gain eternal life through belief in who Jesus is and in what he taught rather than through a sacrificial death on the cross. I was surprised when I discovered that nowhere in the Bible does Jesus say that to get to heaven we must believe in his sacrificial death. This belief was added later in other New Testament books but was not what Jesus taught.

I was also taught that Jesus died on the cross so we could receive forgiveness of our sins. But this makes no sense because the whole time Jesus was alive and interacting with people, he was offering them forgiveness and encouraging them to forgive each other. Therefore, his death on a cross was not necessary for forgiveness. When I consider that God is love, this makes much more sense to me. I have always struggled with the idea of God sacrificing his Son on the cross. In the Old Testament God opposed human sacrifices and the taking of innocent life.

I trust this chapter has caused you to rethink old doctrine as I did when I looked into why Jesus died. I do not expect everyone to agree with my conclusions. I realize the Christian faith is founded on the idea that Jesus died on a cross for our sins so we can receive forgiveness and go to heaven when we die. Much of the Old and New Testaments is connected to this theme, so there is plenty of Scripture to back it up. For this reason, I am not ready to completely abandon this reason for Jesus's death. However, since there are no red-letter words of Jesus in the Bible explaining why he died, I now believe there could be more than one explanation.

> *"The tyrant dies and his rule is over, the martyr dies*
> *and his rule begins" (Soren Kierkegaard).*

Chapter 6

Spiritual Literature

As a Christian I was taught to rely on the Bible as the authority on God and on anything spiritual or supernatural. However, while on this spiritual journey I started reading works from other religious or spiritual orientations and realized there was so much more to learn, some of which aligned with the teachings in the Bible, some of which did not, and some of which brought greater clarity to the biblical message. For the purposes of this book I narrowed all this down to four literary sources: the Bible, the Book of Enoch, the Nag Hammadi Scriptures, and *A Course in Miracles*.

The Bible

Like many of you, I was taught that the Bible is the inerrant Word of God, the only source of truth, nothing missing, every word inspired by God, and that it is the only book we need to read to understand God and to answer all the questions we have about life. So I was surprised a few years ago when God asked me to read the Bible and look for anything that was missing, any contradictions, or things that did not make sense to me. I had never read the Bible this way, so I was unsure of what I would find. Sure enough, I found information missing, contradictions, and things that did not make sense. I have now concluded that the Bible is the foundation on which all truth is based but that it is not the only source of spiritual truth.

The gospel of John concludes by saying, "Jesus did many other things as well. If every one of them were written down, I suppose that even the whole world would not have room for the books that would be written" (John 21:25). Jesus was a controversial figure, so it would make sense that everyone who lived when he did would have something to say about him and that other people, in addition to Matthew, Mark, Luke, and John, would pass things down orally or in written form.

I also had to ask myself how one book could hold everything there is to know about the God who created the universe and everything in it. So I went on a search to find other literature and discovered many writings by people who lived during Old Testament times and also by people who had known Jesus or had lived during his lifetime on earth. These writings gave me a greater understanding of the culture, history, and beliefs of people who lived thousands of years ago. I have found most of it to be complementary rather than contradictory to what is written in the Bible. Some of it was hard to grasp because I had never heard it before and because it took me way out of my spiritual comfort zone. I found errors in my belief system that the Holy Spirit helped me correct.

When I started reading literature outside of the inspired Word of God and the Christian world, I was fearful. What if others saw me buying or reading these books? What would they think? Would they question if I was a real Christian? Would they try to convince me how wrong this was and how I would be led astray and fall into heresy?

Then I had to stop and ask myself why I cared so much about what everyone else thought of me. One day I realized it no longer mattered. My spiritual journey was between myself and God, and I did not need the approval of others. I would listen to their concerns, but ultimately I would follow the leading of the Holy Spirit. As I read, I asked the Spirit to lead me into truth (one of her jobs) and to tell me when I was not reading it, and when she did I quit reading. I also compared what I read with the Bible's teaching to help me understand if it was truth. The more I read, the more I learned and the more my questions were answered, the missing information was found, and the contradictions were explained. I had to ask myself additional questions.

- Why are people so afraid to admit that there is truth outside the Bible?
- Why are we in the church culture encouraged not to seek out additional spiritual truth?
- Why is it so difficult for denominations to admit that some of their beliefs are outdated and no longer relevant?
- Is our denominational truth more important than spiritual truth?
- Why is it so hard to acknowledge that people who do not know Jesus can receive spiritual truth from God?
- Why are we taught that everything must be backed up with a Bible verse before we can believe it?
- Where is all this fear coming from? Jesus taught that as people of love we are not to walk in fear.

I now realize that if you hold up the Bible as the only source of spiritual truth and as the inerrant Word of God, you view the Bible and God from a place of fear rather than of love. You fear that if you admit there could be errors or contradictions in the Bible, you have no guarantee anymore that what you believe is truth. Therefore, you can't trust God, so who or what can you trust? How do you know what is truth? How do you have any assurance that when you die you will go to heaven rather than to hell? Fear now runs rampant in your mind.

God showed me that we have put our faith and trust in a book rather than in a relationship with him. God is so much bigger than the Bible. There is no way one book can contain all of who and what God is. That is one of the reasons Jesus left us the Holy Spirit. It is the Holy Spirit's job to lead us into all truth. But most of us have not been taught through our religious education how to develop a relationship with the Holy Spirit so we can know how to hear and to discern her voice. Rather, we have been taught to rely on our intellectual ability to interpret and to understand the words written in the Bible. While there is nothing wrong with this, we limit ourselves without a relationship with the Holy Spirit to bring enlightenment and truth to everything we read, not just the Bible.

Sometimes I wonder why if what Jesus said was so important, he himself did not write anything down. I understand that in his era, knowledge was passed down through oral communication "as parchment was expensive and few of the early leaders of the church could read or write."[1] I was surprised to learn that there are no original copies of any of the gospels. Since there were no printing presses, it was difficult to create identical copies. Everything had to be handwritten by scribes, with the potential for each to add his own corrections or perspective to what he was writing. The oldest surviving copies date to 175 years after Jesus died, and no two copies are identical to each other.[2] Jesus spoke Aramaic, but the New Testament was composed in Greek because that was the common language of the day. Later it was translated into Latin, then into German, and then into English. Every time the Bible went through a language change, there was a high probability that something from the original was lost and something not previously there was added.

We are told that the writers of the Bible were inspired by God, so we can be assured that what is written is accurate. However, after reading about how the Bible was put together, I now understand how mistakes and mistranslations could easily have occurred. The Spirit showed me that while most of those who wrote and assembled the Bible were inspired by God, the Holy Spirit also brings inspiration to those of us reading the Bible. People can read the same verse and receive different interpretations of what it means. People can read the same passage every year, and the meaning will vary based on where they are in their life journeys. This is why the Bible is sometimes referred to as the living Word. Here are some factors that can influence our understanding of the Bible.

- Different parts of the Bible were written for different audiences and must be understood in context. What was addressed to Jews may not apply to Gentiles. What was addressed to the nations may not apply to an individual person.
- We often make the mistake of reading the Bible with the impression that people then thought and acted like people do today, that their daily interaction with neighbors and family was similar to ours. We forget that this book was written from the perspective of an Eastern mind-set and culture and must be interpreted through this lens and not according to our Western mind-set and culture.
- We tend to read the Bible with the end in mind. When I believe a particular truth, I will interpret everything I read to substantiate this truth. However, when I remove the end result and read with an open mind, I am in a position for the Holy Spirit to reveal alternative ways to understand the Scriptures.

While on my quest to understand the God of love, I have found many Scripture verses that give the impression that God is not love. I used to try to find ways to justify why God appeared to be angry, jealous, divisive, and violent, believing someone could be this way and still be acting from love. The Holy Spirit has shown me that these are not characteristics of love, so they cannot be attributed to God. When we see God portrayed this way in Scripture we have to be careful about how we interpret these verses. Sometimes the writers projected their own feelings onto God or tried to understand God from a limited human perspective. Other times the passage was not translated correctly or must be understood according to the context and the culture in which it was written.

The Holy Spirit suggested that I view the Bible as I view people. Neither has to be perfect to be loved by God or to be used by the Holy Spirit. While God is a perfect being, he does not need perfection in books or in people. Though the Bible has contradictions, missing information, and things that do not make sense, these imperfections do not make it invalid. Rather, they encourage us to draw closer to God to gain understanding. We make mistakes, have misunderstandings, and do not always act kindly toward others, but God works through us and loves us despite these flaws. I have concluded that the Bible is not a perfect document and that I cannot take everything in it literally. I now read the Bible the same way I read any book about spiritual matters—with the guidance of the Holy Spirit.

"The Bible was not given for our information but for our transformation" (D.L. Moody).

The Book of Enoch

Fourteen books are mentioned in the Bible, and the Book of Enoch[3] is one of them. It is the most well-known of the books since it has been published and the others have not. You may be familiar with some of the other books: the Book of Jashar (2 Samuel 1:18), the Annals of Solomon (1 Kings 11:41), the Annals of King David (1 Chronicles 27:24), and the Records of Nathan the Prophet (2 Chronicles 9:29). While these books are mentioned in the Bible, archaeologists have not been able to locate many of these works in archaeological or historical searches.

I knew Enoch was a man mentioned in the Bible, but I had not realized a book was allotted to him. There is little written in the Bible about Enoch other than these verses.

- "When Jared had lived 162 years, he became the father of Enoch" (Genesis 5:19).
- "When Enoch had lived 65 years, he became the father of Methuselah. And after he became the father of Methuselah, Enoch walked with God 300 years and had other sons and daughters. Altogether, Enoch lived 365 years. Enoch walked with God; then he was no more, because God took him away" (Genesis 5:21–24).
- "Enoch, the seventh from Adam, prophesied about these men: 'See, the Lord is coming with thousands upon thousands of his holy ones'" (Jude 1:14).
- "By faith Enoch was taken from this life, so that he did not experience death: he could not be found, because God had taken him away. For before he was taken, he was commended as one who pleased God" (Hebrews 11:5).

If Enoch had enough faith to avoid seeing death, he must have had an incredible understanding of God and of how the spiritual realm operated. What was this knowledge and how did he get it? I was excited when I discovered this book about him since it answered these and many other questions I had.

The Book of Enoch was discovered with the Dead Sea Scrolls and is found in the Bible of the Coptic Christian Church in Ethiopia. It contains three volumes: the Ethiopic Book of Enoch, the Slavonic Secrets of Enoch, and the Hebrew Book of Enoch. The Book of Enoch was written by several authors over a three-hundred-to-four-hundred-year span. Like the four gospel authors writing about Jesus's life, each offered his own interpretation of events. For instance, the stories of creation and of the flood contain similarities and differences.

More than one hundred comments in the New Testament relate to the teachings in the Book of Enoch. Many concepts used by Jesus are connected to terms and ideas in this book. The work is part truth and part myth, so you must be able to discern between these as you read the book. It is not an easy book to read or to understand, but it is fascinating because it provides details missing from the Bible that will challenge what you thought you knew about God. These are the main themes discussed in this book.

- The creation of Adam and Eve
- The fall of the angels to earth
- The consequences for sinners and the righteous
- The lives of Noah and of Methuselah
- The coming Messiah (Jesus) and his judgment
- How the weather, the stars, the planets, the moon, and the calendar were created and how celestial bodies are kept in place
- What the last judgment is
- Visions of Israel's history
- Prophecy about the Apocalypse
- Mystical knowledge about angels, demons, heaven, and hell

Enoch was taken up to heaven several times. The first time he was shown things and given information that he brought back to earth, shared with the people, and wrote down. Later, God told Enoch that he was going to bring Enoch back up again and that he would not be returning to earth, so he needed to convey what he had learned to his family. God stayed true to his word, and Enoch was taken back up to heaven where he remained. Here are a few interesting tidbits from this book.

- Melchizedek was born as his mother was dying. He was born the size of a three-year-old (I assume that was why she died in childbirth) with the badge of the priesthood on his chest. The Lord appeared to his father in a vision to explain that Melchizedek was to be the head of the priests reigning over a royal people who would serve God. When the flood came, an angel took Melchizedek to keep him safe, and he returned to earth after the flood.
- The book discusses the luminaries of heaven (sun, stars, moon, and planets) and the relations of each, according to their names and origins, the months of the seasons, and the laws that will keep them in position until the new creation is completed. I was surprised at how detailed and well-thought-out all of this was and at how specific angels are assigned to keep the celestial order.
- There are ten heavens, and each has a specific purpose and a specific angel monitoring what goes on there. The third heaven is paradise, the home of the tree of life along with many other trees and flowers. Three hundred angels sing continuously as they keep the garden. This is where the righteous live when they leave earth. In the sixth heaven are the archangels. The tenth heaven is where God dwells, with the cherubim and the seraphim singing unceasingly.
- In the highest heaven where God resides, six hundred thousand times ten thousand angels of glory stand over the throne of glory. Innumerable ministering angels carry out God's will. Rivers of joy, streams of gladness, rivers of

happiness, streams of victory, rivers of life, and streams of friendship flow over and out from the throne.

These brief excerpts from the book offer additional information about things we have read in the Bible. Hebrews 7 talks about Melchizedek, Jesus, and the priesthood. The Bible mentions the luminaries that God created, but the Book of Enoch goes into greater detail about their creation and purpose. The Bible uses the word *heaven* in different contexts. We tend to simplify it into one physical location in the spiritual realm, but this book expands the definition of heaven. While the Bible, especially the book of Revelation, talks about angels and the throne of glory, this book gives us a picture of heaven that is humanly possible to comprehend. If you want more detailed information about some of the stories in the Bible, I recommend reading the Book of Enoch.

"It became obvious that the New Testament did not influence the Book of Enoch; on the contrary, the Book of Enoch influenced the New Testament" (Joseph B. Lumpkin).

The Nag Hammadi Scriptures

The Nag Hammadi Scriptures[4] are made up of forty-six texts that were discovered buried in glass jars in a cave in Upper Egypt in 1945. After being researched for authenticity, they were first published in 1977 but were not accessible to the public until 1990. In book form they are quite long—802 pages of small print. Like the Book of Enoch, they contain myths, allegory, and truth, some parts complementary to the Bible and some not found there. The texts contain subject matter similar to what is found in the Book of Enoch and also writings from the disciples and others who interacted with Jesus.

When these texts were written, Jesus had ascended and people were wondering how to interpret his teachings and share them with others. Two basic groups emerged. One group, the orthodox, wanted to organize and control everything and later became known as the church. Leaders of this faction taught that to be a Christian you had to agree to a statement of beliefs or church doctrine. The other group was the Gnostics. They taught that all a person needed to be a Christian was a belief in Jesus, not a statement of beliefs or church doctrine. They encouraged people to question their faith and to seek truth since this was how to grow in a relationship with God. The powerful bishops of the time discredited the Gnostic teachings and referred to adherents as heretics. They had to go underground, and their writings became known as secret teachings. These teachings make up the Nag Hammadi Scriptures. Here is a brief description of some of the texts.

The gospel of Thomas[5] is the most well-known text in these scriptures. It is a collection of the sayings of Jesus rather than the story of his life. Some believe this may be the source material that Matthew, Mark, Luke, and John used when they wrote their gospels, because many statements by Jesus can be found in both places. These sayings should be interpreted in the context of the Aramaic language and culture. Here are a few sayings from this text.

- Jesus said, "I shall give you what no eye has seen and what no ear has heard and what no hand has touched and what has never occurred to the human mind." Interpretation: we cannot use our physical senses to understand spiritual matters.
- Jesus said, "The kingdom of heaven is like a mustard seed. It is the smallest of all seeds. But when it falls on tilled soil, it produces a great plant and becomes a shelter for birds of the sky." Interpretation: truth is like a mustard seed that grows in the minds of those searching for truth.
- Jesus said, "A city being built on a high mountain and fortified cannot fall, nor can it be hidden." Interpretation: a city (the kingdom of heaven on earth), being built on a high mountain (love and truth) and fortified (by perfect faith) cannot fall, nor can it be hidden (due to the light it radiates).
- Jesus said, "Become passers-by." Interpretation: do not form attachments with the things of the world.

The Secret Book of John[6] contains teachings from a post-resurrection discussion between Jesus and John, which may have taken place through a vision, and is a continuation of the book of John in the Bible. John gives Christ a list of questions about who God is and what the eternal realm is like. Jesus shares information about creation, Adam and Eve, and salvation that is similar to what the Book of Enoch offers.

The Revelation of Paul[7] is an allegorical interpretation of what he received from Jesus (Galatians 1:11–17), the revelation he received in the desert (Galatians 2:1–2), and the visions and revelation he received from the Lord (2 Corinthians 12:2–4). Paul writes about his ascension from the third to the tenth heaven (a reference to the Book of Enoch).

The First Revelation of James[8] (the brother of Jesus) is a series of dialogues between James and Jesus. James was fearful over the suffering Jesus was about to endure on the cross. Jesus discussed this with James and prepared him for his own future suffering through martyrdom.

In the Revelation of Peter,[9] Jesus tells him the meaning of the crucifixion and the nature of genuine Christianity. Jesus speaks to Peter in a vision. This information will cause you to question what you have been taught about the crucifixion.

The letter of Peter to Philip[10] details a discussion Jesus had with the disciples after his resurrection when he appeared to them as a great light. Jesus encourages them to teach salvation, to arm themselves with the power of God, and not to be afraid. As in the Acts of the Apostles, the letter recounts Peter preaching on Pentecost.

The gospel of Mary[11] is the only gospel ascribed to a woman and gives an account of a post-resurrection appearance of Jesus to his disciples. Jesus had given Mary Magdalene spiritual knowledge through a vision. There is a dispute between Mary and Peter because she appears to have more spiritual insight, but she is a woman, so Peter does not understand why Jesus would give this information to her rather than to him. Peter puts greater priority on the physical body and on gender than on spiritual truth. Jesus gives a teaching on the meaning of sin that offers a different perspective than what we have been taught in church.

The gospel of Judas[12] was not discovered until the 1970s and was first published in 2006. It contains a discussion between Jesus and Judas shortly before the crucifixion and differs from what we have been taught in the church. According to this account, Jesus and Judas were good friends, and Jesus explained to Judas why it was a spiritual necessity that he betray Jesus.

The Nag Hammadi Scriptures are controversial among Christians due to content that sometimes contradicts what is in the Bible. It is also difficult at times to discern how to interpret these books given the amount of myth and allegory interspersed with truth. However, I do not think we should let fear prevent us from reading sources that provide new insights into the life of Jesus and what the Bible says. None of us has all truth, and I believe that truth is scattered in many places. With the assistance of the Holy Spirit, people can discern the truth within this book.

> *"Know what is in front of your face, and what is hidden from you will be disclosed to you. For there is nothing hidden that will not be revealed" (Gospel of Thomas).*

A Course in Miracles

A Course in Miracles[13] (ACIM) was one of those books I was told by Christians not to read. I am so thankful I did not listen to them and read it anyway. Other than the Bible, this is probably the most important book I have ever read related to spirituality. More than anything else it helped me understand the concept of living from fear rather than from love, which is what God is. The book in its complete edition is 1,295 pages and took me two years to read because there was so much to digest in each verse. It reports the words of Jesus given over a seven-year period to an atheist named Helen Schucman and her coworker William Thetford, who were professors of medical psychology.

At first I wondered why God would choose to give spiritual truth to an atheist, and when I asked God he told me he could not give it to religious people because they would interpret everything Jesus said through their own belief systems. An atheist like Schucman, with no spiritual belief system, would write down whatever Jesus told her, because she would not be interested in interpreting or understanding anything. Brilliant, God.

In this book Jesus takes Bible verses and beliefs taught in church and shows us how they are based on fear and how to interpret them from a place of love, the original intent when they were given. The book teaches us how to apply the teachings of Jesus through our life experiences rather than focusing solely on theology. It helps people sort through their perceptions, illusions, and ignorance about life and spiritual issues and to discover what reality and truth really are. We live our lives caught between illusion and reality and don't always know how to differentiate between them. Some of the topics the book addresses are atonement, the ego, healing and wholeness, love, God, the Holy Spirt, truth, forgiveness, peace, salvation, justice, and fear. Here are some quotes from this book.

- "'I will visit the sins of the fathers unto the third and fourth generation' means that 'in later generations the Holy

Spirit can still reinterpret what former generations had misunderstood, and thus release the thoughts from the ability to produce fear.'"[14]

- "'Many are called but few are chosen' should be 'All are called but few choose to listen.'"[15]

- "'Heaven and earth shall pass away' means that 'they will not continue to exist as separate states. My word, which is the resurrection and the life, shall not pass away because life is eternal. You are the work of God and His work is wholly lovable and wholly loving. This is how man must think of himself in his heart, because this is what he is.'"[16]

- "'God is not partial' means 'all His children have His total love, and all His gifts are freely given to everyone alike.'"[17]

- "'Except ye become as little children' means that 'unless you fully recognize your complete dependence on God you cannot know the real power of the Son in his true relationship with the father.'"[18]

- "'God so loved the world that he *gave it to* his only begotten Son.' The Bible version says 'God so loved the world that he *gave his* only begotten son' (italics mine). Two words, *it to*, can change the meaning."[19]

- "The message of the crucifixion is perfectly clear: Teach only love, for this is what you are. If you interpret the crucifixion in any other way, you are using it as a weapon for assault rather than as a call for peace for which it was intended. The apostles often misunderstood it, and for the same reason that anyone misunderstands it. Their own imperfect love made them vulnerable to projection and out of their own fear they spoke of the 'wrath of God' as His retaliatory weapon. Nor could they speak of the crucifixion entirely without anger, because their sense of guilt had made them angry. These are some of the examples of upside-down thinking in the New Testament, although its gospel is really only the message of love."[20]

- "The Last Judgment is generally thought of as a procedure undertaken by God. Actually it will be undertaken by my brothers with my help. It is a final healing rather than a meting out of punishment however much you may think that punishment is desired. Punishment is a concept totally opposed to rightmindedness and the aim of the Last Judgment is to restore rightmindedness to you. The Last Judgment might be called a process of right evaluation. It simply means that everyone will finally come to understand what is worthy and what is not."[21]
- "Offer your brother the gift of lilies, not the crown of thorns; the gift of love and not the gift of fear."[22]
- "The mind is very powerful, and never loses its creative force. It never sleeps. Every instant it is creating."[23]
- "Easter is not the celebration of the cost of sin but of its end."[24]
- "Nothing can hurt you unless you give it the power to do so."[25]
- "Trials are but lessons that you failed to learn presented once again, so where you made a faulty choice before you now can make a better one, and thus escape all pain that what you chose before has brought to you."[26]
- "You who believe that sacrifice is love must learn that sacrifice is separation from love."[27]
- "Your task is not to seek for love, but merely to seek and find all the barriers within yourself that you have built against it."[28]

The greatest lesson I learned from this book was that everything God created is perfect because he creates and sustains it by love. Anytime people choose fear over love, they have the wrong perception and are living in ignorance. This creates the conflict and division we see within ourselves, our families, and the world around us. Sin is a loveless perception. Jesus gave us the Holy Spirit to help us mediate between the world of love and the world of fear, to help

Chapter 7

Beliefs

What we believe tells a lot about who we are and how we interpret the world around and beyond us. It is also what often separates us from other religions and causes wars to break out among us. When we don't understand what others believe, we tend to fear them and either want nothing to do with them or would like to be friends but do not know how to build relationships with them. In this chapter I will discuss what a belief is, my definition of a Christian, and the beliefs of Gnostics, the New Age movement, and other religions.

Beliefs

As Christians we should be the most knowledgeable people on the planet about the spiritual realm, but unfortunately we are some of the least knowledgeable. Why is this? We say we believe in God, Jesus, the Holy Spirit, angels, and heaven, but we have only limited knowledge about these topics. This is because we do not allow ourselves to go outside the Bible or traditional Christian thought for information. When I stepped out of the Bible bubble years ago and began reading from other sources and listening to and interacting with scientists, healers, spiritual teachers, and others, I purposely stayed away from those who called themselves Christians. I wanted to know how everyone else understood and experienced the spiritual world.

I discovered a whole other world I had known little about, and yet much of it correlated with the teachings of Jesus. I had to review what I believed and why I believed these things. I had been taught that Jesus was the only way to God and that no one could know God without first having a relationship with Jesus. And yet the people I was learning about or meeting all had amazing relationships with God and were full of love and forgiveness to an extent I had rarely witnessed in the church. Many believed in Jesus and lived out his teachings but did not call themselves Christians or attend church. How could this be? It went against everything I had been taught.

I had to reevaluate things. I discovered there was nothing inherently wrong in the Bible. The problem was our often-inaccurate interpretation of the Bible's stories and teachings. Anytime we read or experience something, we interpret it based on where we are at that moment, our personal perceptions, experiences, culture, knowledge, and fears. Then we try to convince others that we have the truth, the accurate interpretation. I have been going back through the Bible, asking the Holy Spirit to point out the errors in my belief system, and then letting them go.

In the church we talk about everyone having a personal relationship with Jesus and God, and yet when we choose to disagree with the majority belief system, we are told we are not real Christians. To me, a personal relationship means that where I am with God will change from day to day, just as it does in my human relationships. My relationship will not look like yours, and that is okay. The Holy Spirit has showed me that many of our Christian beliefs are rooted in fear rather than in love. Since God is love, everything we do and believe as his children must be based on love and not on fear.

Christians can get entangled with beliefs and doctrines. Doctrines are generally the beliefs on which a denomination agrees and that differentiate it from all the others. Beliefs are what we as individuals hold true about our Christian faith. We are encouraged not to question doctrines or beliefs, because the people who originally declared them heard from God and understood accurately how to interpret Scripture. We are encouraged to hang on to these beliefs since they are the foundational truths on which everything else stands. We are not always encouraged to think for ourselves, to question, to set aside our fears, and to look beyond what we have been taught. Do our relationships and our security depend more on our belief system than on our God?

Some people like to have what they believe figured out for them by others in an easily understandable format. Even if some things may not seem right, these people do not question them, because they have been taught to accept everything on faith. When someone challenges what they believe they may become defensive and hang on even more tightly to their belief systems. Other people have a foundational belief system, but they keep it flexible so they can make adjustments as additional information, discoveries, and revelations come forth. They realize it would be impossible for one person, church, or denomination to have all truth. When someone challenges them, rather than feel threatened, they ask questions and are curious about what this other person believes even if they disagree. Most people are somewhere between these two examples. Where you are depends on your personality, your religious upbringing, and your life experiences.

The Holy Spirit showed me that our beliefs and doctrines can become like idols in our lives. We fear changing them, so even when we know they no longer serve us and are outdated, we cling to them, caring more about being accepted by people and the church than about changing our beliefs based on new information. We let our fears rather than God's love determine what we believe. We define ourselves by our beliefs and doctrines rather by who God says we are. We confuse beliefs and doctrine with truth. We believe the lie that unity means everyone must believe the same thing. I believe unity actually means we can all come together with our varying beliefs and choose to love and respect each other anyway. Think of a symphony in which each of us is a different instrument but we can still play together to make beautiful music. When we are confident in who we are and what we believe we will no longer become defensive or be offended by people who hold beliefs different from our own.

When we are growing spiritually, our beliefs should grow and evolve. Every time we learn new information or have a new experience that will affect our beliefs. A belief is not something set in stone. It is something that guides us through life. People previously believed the earth was flat but had to change that belief based on new information. People believed that women should not work, but now they work. Do not fear changing your beliefs as you experience more of life. Truth, on the other hand, is unchangeable and set in stone. So what is truth? The answer will depend on whom you ask. I would say the truth is that God, Jesus, and the Holy Spirit are real, that the spiritual realm is more real than the physical world, and that love is the ultimate truth.

> *"An old belief is like an old shoe. We so value its comfort that we fail to notice the hole in it." (Robert Brault)*

Christians

One of the world's major belief systems is Christianity. Those of us who adhere to this belief system are often referred to as Christians. One day the Holy Spirit asked me what a Christian was. I gave her the standard answer—someone who has accepted Jesus as Lord and Savior. Then she showed me all the judgments we make against people; maybe you are familiar with a few of these. People cannot be Christians because:

- They do not go to church anymore.
- They are alcoholics or drug addicts.
- They do not tithe.
- They had an affair.
- They are divorced.
- They are homosexuals.
- They are Democrats.
- They believe in UFOs.
- They believe in reincarnation.
- They are such critical, negative persons.
- They are on their fourth marriage.
- They have never been baptized in water.
- They have never received the baptism of the Holy Spirit with tongues.

I realized how we have added to the simple definition of what a Christian is and used this against people. So I had to rethink what a Christian is from God's perspective. I found the word *Christian* mentioned only three times in the Bible, in the following verses.

- "And when he found him, he brought him to Antioch. So for a whole year Barnabas and Saul met with the church and taught great numbers of people. The disciples were called Christians first at Antioch" (Acts 11:26).

- "Then Agrippa said to Paul, 'Do you think that in such a short time you can persuade me to be a Christian?'" (Acts 26:28).
- "However, if you suffer as a Christian, do not be ashamed, but praise God that you bear that name" (1 Peter 4:16).

None of these verses defines what a Christian is. So here is my definition: someone who believes that Jesus is who he claims to be. When we define a Christian by behaviors, we step out of grace and into law and legalism. Jesus made it simple: we have only one law to live by: love God, self, and others. We are all at different places when we choose to believe in Jesus, so our spiritual journeys will all be different. As we grow in our love and understanding of God, the Holy Spirit will show us how God sees us through Jesus. As we begin to believe that we are forgiven, loved, worthy, protected, free, perfect, and desired by God, we will no longer want to live a lifestyle in opposition to who we really are. The sins of the past will begin to fade away as the Holy Spirit takes us through the transformation process to be more like Jesus. Of course, due to our free will, we can choose to remain as we are and not to be transformed. The amazing thing is that God's love for us will not change regardless of which choice we make. What will change is how far or how close we feel to God. The more we align our lives up with who God says we are, the closer we will feel to him.

I believe there are far more Christians on the planet than the church realizes, because many people who believe in Jesus do not feel welcomed in the average church. We tell them, "Come as you are. Jesus loves you just as you are." Then when they show up we tell them how they have to change their beliefs and their lifestyles and give them a list of things they must abide by to be real Christians. We take on the role of the Holy Spirit in their lives instead of teaching them how to hear from God for themselves and loving them as they are. My prayer is that we can all stop putting labels on people and learn to love and to appreciate them for who they are, what they believe, and where they are in their life journeys.

> *"I like your Christ, I do not like your Christians. Your Christians are so unlike your Christ." (Mahatma Gandhi)*

Gnostics

When people talk about Christianity they have a common understanding about the basic doctrinal beliefs on which the faith is founded. Reading the Nag Hammadi Scriptures was my first exposure to another group of Christians referred to as Gnostic whose beliefs differed from the traditional Christianity I was taught. Prior to this, I had never heard the term *Gnostic* and knew nothing about it. I looked it up online and found many Christian sites saying Gnostic beliefs were heresy and should be rejected because they were contrary to biblical Scripture. This just got my curiosity up, so I did the opposite and read everything I could on Gnostics. One of my favorite books was *The Gnostic Gospels*[1] by Elaine Pagles. The purpose of her book was not to convince readers to accept or to reject Gnosticism but to give them the facts so they could make up their own minds. What I found was fascinating, so I will briefly share what I learned.

After Jesus ascended to heaven, the disciples were unsure of what to do. Their leader was gone and they needed to decide the best way to share his life and his truth with the world. Initially, all members of the Christian community held their money and property in common, believed the same teachings, and worshiped together, revering the authority of the apostles. However, this peace did not last, and division began between numerous groups of people who interpreted the life, teachings, and death of Jesus differently and had conflicting opinions on who should lead the Christian movement. Out of this confusion came two basic groups, the orthodox and the Gnostics. Both claimed that they were the true Christians and "accused each other of being outsiders, false brethren and hypocrites."[2]

The orthodox believed that the only ones who could lead this new movement were the disciples since they had been eyewitnesses to Jesus and had enjoyed personal relationships with him while he was alive. Members of this faction believed they needed to find some way to unify and to control everyone, so they agreed upon basic doctrines about Jesus and labeled them truth. They formed a hierarchical structure of leadership to oversee all the local churches. They took the teachings and the life of Jesus literally and did not look for the deeper spiritual meanings behind what he taught. Experiencing new birth meant acknowledging and repenting of sin and receiving what Christ did on the cross for them. The orthodox believed that since Christ suffered and died, his followers would also experience suffering and possible martyrdom so they could fully understand what Christ endured for them.

Gnostics believed that a person did not have to be an eyewitness to Jesus or to have had a personal relationship with him while he was alive to lead this new movement. They believed that people could be unified by having common understandings about Jesus but that they should be left to interpret teachings in a way that was meaningful to them. They believed that a personal relationship with Jesus meant just that—people could converse with him through the Holy Spirit and did not need any church hierarchical leadership or doctrines to tell them what to do and to believe. They did not take the teachings and the life of Jesus literally but looked for the deeper spiritual meanings behind what Jesus taught. Gnostics believed no one person or one religion could possess or know all truth. They each had parts of the truth, and there were things to learn from them all. Gnostics believed Christ suffered and died for them so they might not suffer and die as he did. For them, martyrdom was a foolish waste of human life. Christ had died to set them free from this. Martyrdom was considered a form of human sacrifice that God opposed.

Because the orthodox group was highly structured and organized and the Gnostics were not, orthodox beliefs came to dominate. Emperor Constantine made Christianity an officially approved religion in the fourth century.[3] Christianity was now an institution headed by bishops, priests, and deacons who rejected all other viewpoints as heresy, insisting there could be only one church, the orthodox Catholic Church. Any books written from a Gnostic perspective were labeled heretical, and possessing one could be a criminal offense. When these books were found, they were destroyed. Many Gnostic believers went into hiding, and monks hid some of the books in a jar where they remained buried for almost 1,600 years.[4] In 1945, these writings were discovered and are now the Nag Hammadi Scriptures.[5]

After comparing these two viewpoints, I found things I agreed and disagreed with in both faith traditions, but I would say that I lean more toward the Gnostic than the orthodox beliefs. They seem to me to show a better understanding of Jesus's teachings about love and how this love is supposed to be lived out.

"Gnosticism and orthodoxy, then, articulated very different kinds of human experiences; I suspect that they appealed to different types of persons" (Elaine Pagels).

The New Age Movement

I was in high school when the New Age movement began infiltrating America from other countries. I was told at the time that New Age beliefs conflicted with Christianity and that I should stay away from anything associated with the movement. I did until ten years ago when I started looking into New Age healing methods and discovered they worked. I wrote about this in my book *Interconnected by God: Healing for Your Spirit, Soul and Body.*

New Age teachings became popular in America during the 1970s. They are rooted in Eastern mysticism, Gnostic teachings, modern philosophy, psychology, and science. New Age is not considered a religion but a movement because it has no spiritual book to guide it, no organizational structure, no membership requirements, no clergy, no monetary requirements, and no dogma. It is a loose network of people who share similar beliefs and lifestyle practices. Since this movement is so individualized how people practice it can vary enormously. Some things often associated with it are meditation, yoga, crystals, tarot cards, astrology, numerology, acupuncture, massage, healing touch, reflexology, channeling, psychic communication, candles, chanting, and music.

New Age followers use different terminology than Christians do, so at first glance it may seem like the two groups have little in common. Here are some New Age beliefs and my comments about how they compare with Christian beliefs.

New Age Beliefs	Comparison with Christian Beliefs
God – Everything that exists comes from a single source of divine energy. God is all that exists. God is the entire universe but transcends the universe as well. God is the one universal mind, the cosmic consciousness, the universal presence or force. Therefore, God is impersonal. God has no gender and so can be referred to as a he or a she.	Genesis tells us God is the sole creator of everything. If that is so, then his presence, his DNA, his spirit are in everything he created, just as our children have a part of ourselves in them. The idea of an impersonal God is not universal. Many people with New Age beliefs say they have a personal relationship with God. I agree that the gender of God is neutral, a balance of feminine and masculine.
Reincarnation – Because their souls are eternal, when people die they can return to earth in new bodies and live through many other lifetimes.	Christians agree that souls are eternal but believe they only live one lifetime on earth and then they live permanently in heaven or hell.
Karma – Also referred to as the law of attraction. If you sow evil, you will reap evil; if you sow good, good will come to you. Some believe karma can be reversed through reincarnation.	Jesus spoke many times about the law of sowing and reaping, giving and receiving, and treating others as you would want to be treated.

Auras – People are made up of energy and radiate auras or energy fields around their bodies.	Science has proved this to be true. At our core we are all made up of electromagnetic energy vibrating at different frequencies. Many verses in the Bible talk about a presence of light, the light within us, and the glory seen around people.
Personal transformation – Using energy treatments, meditation, spiritual experiences, and psychic power, people can bring about spiritual, emotional, and physical healing in their bodies, souls, and spirits.	Jesus spoke quite a bit about personal transformation, saying that we are to become spiritually mature, that we are to remove the ways of the flesh and to be ruled by the spirit, that we are to be healthy, not sick.
Nature – Everything was created by God and so contains his life force. Thus we must honor and care for nature. New Agers often refer to earth as Gaia or Mother Earth. Some would make man and nature of equal value. They believe that there is much we can learn from the animal and plant world and that we are to live in harmony with this world.	Sometimes I do not think we Christians honor the creation God blessed us with as much as we should. We misinterpret dominion over it to mean we can do whatever we want as opposed to caring for and preserving nature. The balance is to appreciate and to care for nature but not to worship it.

New world – New Agers believe that as love increases around the world, fear will decrease, and the vibrational frequency of the planet will increase to the point where love, joy, and peace will dominate and there will be an end to war, disease, discrimination, hunger, pollution, and poverty. People will no longer compete against each other but will realize they are all one and will learn how to cooperate.	Jesus often spoke about unity and working together and about how there would be a day when peace would reign and fear would vanish and the lion would lie down with the lamb. So Christians agree with the concept of a new world, but the timing and how it will take place differ from New Age thought.
Good and evil – New Agers believe in the existence of evil and sin but do not focus on this, believing goodness and love are strong enough to overcome evil and sin when people put their energy into practice and live out goodness and love.	While Christians agree that good can overcome evil and this is a biblical concept, we believe that you need Jesus and the power of the Holy Spirit to make this happen, while New Agers would say a belief in God is all you need.

Spiritual communication – People have the ability to access spiritual information and power directly from God, angels, spirit guides, and other spiritual beings of light through prayer, meditation, channeling, astrology, palm reading, and psychic powers.	Christians agree that we all have the ability to access spiritual information and power from God through Jesus, the Holy Spirit, angels, and prayer. However, Christians also believe discernment is needed since information can also come through demonic sources.
Man can become like God; I am God – Since people are created by God, they have his spirit and presence within them. The goal of life is to expand upon this presence so we have God's attributes and can operate from love, joy, and peace rather than from fear and judgment.	We can never become God, so the "I am God" statement is false, but we are encouraged by Jesus to become like God, taking on his attributes just as Jesus did.
Jesus – Beliefs vary depending on the person. Most New Agers believe that Jesus is the Son of God and that he was a great teacher who came to give us the message of love. They do not believe Jesus came to die for our sins, and they do not agree that he is the only person God sent to earth to bring spiritual truth.	Christians believe that Jesus is the son of God, is the greatest spiritual teacher and came to earth to die for our sins so we could go to heaven rather than hell when we die.

Morality –- New Agers do not have any written moral laws they abide by. They believe love rather than law should motivate action.	Christians generally agree that a moral code and laws are very important to live our lives by.

I have found there is much we can learn from New Age beliefs and practices. This movement is not something Christians need to fear. What is most important when dealing with anything spiritual is to discern the source. There are only two sources of spiritual knowledge and experience—God (love) and Satan (fear). Ask the Holy Spirit for discernment, and you will be able to know what is okay for you to use and to believe and what is not.

Namaste
The Divine light in me acknowledges the Divine light in you
We are all created from the same One Divine Consciousness of God

Religions

I had always been taught that Jesus was the only way to God and that Christianity was the only true religion. Christians were required by God to do whatever they could to convert people to Christianity so they would not go to hell when they died. But when I looked at a God of love, I struggled with this teaching because it did not sound or feel like love to me. I saw that God had created a world full of diversity: thousands of species of animals, fish, and plants and many peoples and cultures—all of them unique and special and yet all of them interconnected and dependent on each other for life and love. So why would God be so diverse in all of his creation and yet offer only one way to connect with him?

Every religion has false beliefs within it because every religion was created by imperfect people incapable of completely understanding God. Every religion also has true beliefs within it because every religion has people who are genuinely seeking God, and when you seek God you will find him and his truth. When people claim that their religion is the only truth, they place themselves above others and become prideful, believing they are somehow better than others, more spiritual, or superior in some way. This then creates division and conflict. People are no longer seen as fellow creatures to love but as targets to convert. Christians greatly fear that their loved ones will not get saved in time and will end up in hell. Churches challenge Christians and congregations to see how many people they can convert each week or bring to church. Churches hold contests, encouraging people to compete against each other for the prize of telling the most people about Jesus in a week or a month. I never read about Jesus acting this way in the Bible.

God wants all of his children to realize that they are not alone, that there is a God who created and loves them and wants to have a relationship with them. There are no limitations on how God can choose to connect with his creation, which is why so many roads lead to him. It does not matter which road we choose as long as we find one that will take us to God and will affirm his great love for us. I have chosen Christianity because I am drawn to the teachings of Jesus about love, and this is what resonates most deeply within me. If I had been raised in a different culture, I might have chosen something else. I believe our goal as people of faith is to lead others to God so they can develop a relationship with him, fully enjoy their lives on earth, and know that an afterlife awaits them.

Jesus said, "I am the way, and the truth and the life. No one comes to the Father except through me" (John 14:6), and Christians use this verse to claim that theirs is the only true religion and that the only way to God is through Jesus. However, I have found many people who have experienced love, peace, joy, and a relationship with God without going through Jesus. Scientific studies have identified non-Christians who have had near-death and out-of-body experiences and have found themselves in the light of God rather than in the darkness of hell.

When I learn about personal experiences and scientific information contradicting what the Bible says, I have to conclude that the words spoken by Jesus were changed and edited through numerous translations or have been misinterpreted. I believe the verse above means that *no one comes to the full knowledge of the Father God except through the teachings of Jesus, which are all about love.* Many spiritual teachers before and after Jesus have taught this message of love. However, because Jesus was God's Son and was present with God when everything was created, I will always hold him above any other spiritual teacher or leader.

When you compare the core beliefs of the major world religions, you find they have much in common: love, a belief in God and the spiritual realm and in the interconnectedness of life. They have different ways of expressing these beliefs based on culture and history. I prefer to focus on what we have in common rather than on our differences. I believe this is what love would do. Here are some beliefs we share.

Common Belief	How It Is Expressed
There is only one God.	• "The Lord is our God. The Lord is one" (Hebrew prayer). • "Allah is one" (Qur'an). • "There is only one God" (Chief Seattle).
God is everywhere.	• "The whole world is Brahman" (Hinduism). • "The earth is full of His unfailing love" (Psalm 33:5). • "We think of Tirawa (God) as in everything" (Lenape Indian).
The soul is eternal.	• "Do not be afraid of those who kill the body but cannot kill the soul" (Matthew 10:28). • "A soul will not die" (Qur'an). • "For the soul there is never birth nor death. It is not slain when the body is slain" (Hinduism).
God lives within us.	• "God dwelleth in all hearts" (Bhagavad Gita). • "All animals have power because the Great Spirit dwells in all of them" (Lame Deer, Sioux Chief). • "The kingdom of God is within you" (Luke 17:21).

Compassion and respect for everyone	• "All beings long for happiness. Therefore extend thy compassion to all. He who wishes his own happiness, let him cultivate good will toward all the world" (Buddha). • "Love your enemies and pray for those who persecute you" (Matthew 5:44) • "Judge everybody favorably" (The Talmud, a sacred Jewish book).
Spiritual knowledge is accessible to everyone.	• "All who dwell on earth may find you" (Jewish prayer book). • "Seek knowledge from the cradle to the grave" (Muhammad). • "Search with sincerity and in the end you will find the truth" (Buddha).
The interconnectedness of all	• "All creatures are members of the one family of God" (Muhammad). • "One thing we know. All men are brothers" (Chief Seattle). • "All people are your children, whatever their belief, whatever their shade of skin" (Jewish prayer book).

Peace and nonviolence	<ul><li>"And make not Allah an obstacle to your doing good and guarding against evil and making peace between men" (Qur'an).</li><li>"Nonviolence, absence of anger, equanimity, abstaining from malicious talk, compassion for all creatures, gentleness, forgiveness, absence of malice, and absence of pride—these are some of the qualities of those endowed with divine virtues" (Bhagavad-Gita).</li><li>"May your children unite and do your will: to establish peace and justice throughout the world, so that nations are drawn together by the bond of friendship" (Jewish prayer book).</li></ul>

The Golden Rule	<ul><li>"Do to others what you would have them do to you" (Matthew 7:12).</li><li>"What is hurtful to yourself do not do to your fellow man. This is the whole of the Torah and the remainder is but commentary" (Judaism).</li><li>"Do unto all men as you would they should unto you, and reject for others what you would reject for yourself" (Islam).</li><li>"Hurt not others with that which pains yourself" (Buddhism).</li><li>"Tzu King asked, 'Is there any one principle upon which one's whole life may proceed?' Confucius replied, 'Is not reciprocity such a principle? What you do not yourself desire, do not put before others'" (Confucianism).</li><li>"This is the sum of all true righteousness: Treat others, as thou wouldst thyself be treated. Do nothing to thy neighbor, which hereafter thou wouldst not have thy neighbor do to thee" (Hinduism).</li><li>"Treat others as thou wouldst be treated thyself" (Sikhism).</li><li>"Regard your neighbor's gain as your own gain; and regard your neighbor's loss as your own loss, even as though you were in their place" (Taoism).</li></ul>

	• "Ascribe not to any soul that which thou wouldst not have ascribed to thee" (Baha'i).
Morals	• The Ten Commandments (Exodus 20:1–17) • The Ten Precepts (Buddha)

I believe religions were not created by God but were created by man. From the beginning of time man has known there was something beyond this earth; a spiritual connection, a moral code, a God of some kind existed. Every culture created a way to express and to define these ideas, which became known as religions. These religions were then given hierarchy and structure to try to bring unity among followers and to control the people through one common, agreed-upon belief system. When Jesus was alive, many religions had long existed, and yet he never warned people to avoid certain ones or their beliefs. I do not believe any of them has all the truth, but they all have parts of it, and if we can let go of our fears and replace them with love, understanding, and respect, we will find much to learn from the different religions. I believe when we get to heaven we will see people from all religions and belief systems because God looks at the heart or the intent of a person, whether someone was motivated by love or by fear, rather than the person's religious affiliation.

"Love removes all the dross from man, and saves all.
Love is the ultimate religion. Classify me not by creed: I
belong to nothing but love"[6] (Toyohiko Kagawa).

Chapter 8

The Spiritual Realm

For much of my life I thought I understood the spiritual realm. It consisted of heaven, hell, angels, and demons. When I became a psychotherapist and started exploring alternative healing methods, I discovered a new world. I want to introduce this world to you since you may be where I was, letting fear prevent you from going beyond traditional Christian thinking on these topics. In this chapter I discuss the human energy system, the oneness of everything, extraterrestrial life, reincarnation, death and dying, the demonic, and what life is like when we cross over to the other side at death.

The Human Energy System

As a psychotherapist I started learning about alternative therapies when I was looking for something that would be more effective than traditional therapeutic treatments at helping clients overcome trauma and past abuse. Initially I feared venturing into this world since I had been told these therapies were not evidenced-based and came out of Eastern mysticism. I discovered the world of energy—how all of us are made up of energy, how we can use energy to heal people, and how energy is connected to the spiritual realm. I realized this was the way Jesus healed when he laid hands on people. I wrote about this in my previous book, *Interconnected by God: Healing for Your Spirit, Soul and Body*. In this essay I will offer a brief overview of the human energy system, what the parts are, and how they work together to keep you healthy in body, soul, and spirit.

Everyone has a physical body and an energy or spiritual body. These two bodies work together to keep you healthy and enable you to communicate with the spiritual realm. Scientists have discovered the universe is made up of little building blocks, extremely small particles of light called bio photons. These bio photons enable people to communicate within their own body systems, with the environment around their bodies, and with the spiritual realm.

Since nothing God creates is identical to anything else, every material structure in the universe, including people, radiates its own unique energy signature, which is constantly spinning and vibrating.[1] This energy spins so rapidly you are unaware of it moving within you. Just as no one notices the world spinning on its axis, people go through life unaware of this vibrating energy within and around them. However, people can develop the ability to read, feel, interact with, and interpret this energy.

This energy vibrates at different frequencies within the body, soul, and spirit from very low to very high. When people are living in low, dense vibrational frequencies they will experience things such as sickness, fear, anxiety, depression, guilt, shame, lack, unforgiveness, anger, and hate. When people are living in high, light vibrational frequencies they will experience health, peace, joy, abundance, confidence, gratitude, forgiveness, and love. The good news is that many things can be done to raise these frequencies.

- *Monitor your thoughts.* Thoughts are powerful energy forces that can change your life. Research has shown that around 87 percent of illness can be attributed to our thought life, not to genetics or to diet.[2] Take time to listen to the thoughts you think and the words you say. Are they more positive or negative? If they lean toward the negative, start making a conscious effort to notice negative thoughts and find a way to change them into positive statements.
- *Monitor your emotions.* Emotions are also powerful and are rooted in fear or in love. Take time to become aware of your feelings. If they lean toward depression, anxiety, fear, guilt, or anger, allow yourself to experience and to appropriately release these feelings so they don't get trapped inside of you.
- *Rocks, crystals, and minerals.* Many people claim healing can come from wearing these on their bodies or having them in their homes. Studies show that electromagnetic radiation from crystals affects the bio photons in the body. Each rock, crystal, and mineral vibrates at a different level and is used to heal different things. Many verses in the Bible talk about precious stones being used for a variety of purposes (Exodus 28:17–21, 1 Chronicles 29:2, Revelation 21:18–21).
- *Plants, herbs, and essential oils.* Herbs have been safely used for thousands of years on their own and in pharmaceutical drugs or natural supplements. They help the body repair and regenerate damaged tissue and facilitate biochemical activity at the cellular level. Plants and essential oils have their own vibrational frequencies. Essential oils have coherent frequencies that harmonize and heal the electrical field of the body. Eating healthy foods is also important.

White sugars, refined white flour, preservatives, chemicals, and fried food all have very low frequencies, so you want to avoid them.

- *Massage and exercise.* These healing tools directly affect the body. Exercise will get the blood flowing and increase your energy level, raising your frequencies. It moves energy through the body and around your aura. Any type of exercise or movement will work, so you can run, walk, dance, swim, or do martial arts. Massage and touch increase the endorphins to your brain, enabling you to relax and to feel pleasure and enjoyment. Massage releases energy blocks in your meridian system, allowing the energy to flow again.
- *Music and sound.* Music composed of harmonic frequencies tends to pull subatomic particles together, meaning it may help you feel good and increase health. Discordant frequencies will tend to split or to explode the particles, meaning you may not feel very good and your health may be harmed. Sounds correlate with your emotions, so music can have a strong impact on how you feel. This is why spending time in worship can be such a powerful experience. Worship raises your frequencies to align with the frequency of the Holy Spirit so you can feel and connect with the presence of God.
- *Beauty, nature, and pets.* Beauty and nature vibrate at higher frequencies, and you can absorb some of those frequencies into your being by spending time in beautiful spaces or with nature. Pets are known for their unconditional love, one of the highest frequencies, which is why pets can help calm people.
- *Mindfulness, meditation, gratitude, and prayer.* All of these practices help you learn how to calm your busy mind, take your mind off of your problems, and focus on the spiritual so you can connect with God, the highest vibrational frequency.
- *Healthy people.* These people regularly operate at higher frequencies, and you will automatically raise your frequencies

just by being around them. They encourage you, love you unconditionally, have a good sense of humor, and enjoy life. Avoid spending time with negative, critical people, who will lower your frequencies.

- *Be love.* Love is the highest vibration you can have, because it is who God is. So always forgive, show kindness, and love every chance you get.

Another part of the energy system is the cytoskeleton, the connective tissue system that processes and conveys information to every part of the body, much like the semiconductor chips in a computer.[3] Every thought you have echoes through this connective tissue and turns genes on and off, producing either a stress or a healing response in your body.[4] This provides the semiconductive electrical circuitry called the Chinese meridian system. The main governing meridian line runs along the spine with many other lines branching off of this one. The meridian lines carry energy throughout the body much like arteries carry blood throughout the body. On the skin are acupoints that connect hundreds of tiny, distinct reservoirs of heat and electromagnetic energy along the surface.[5] When stimulated these points remove physical and emotional pain from the body and the subconscious mind. When the energy lines and points are blocked, people become sick; when they are open and flowing, people are in good health.

Along the center of the body from the top of the head to the base of the spine are seven centers of electromagnetic activity referred to as energy stations or chakras. These store emotional memories from the nearest organ and influence the health of that organ. Like meridians and points, they can be open or blocked. They each have their own name, color, frequency rate, and purpose.

Around the body is an aura—also called a spirit, a biofield, or an orb—that protects your energy system in the same way skin protects your organs. All the photons emitted from the body communicate with each other instantly in this highly structured energy field surrounding the body. Researchers have discovered that "all organisms, including humans, communicate and read their environment by evaluating energy fields."[6] Today the majority of people do not use this communication since they have become dependent on their five senses (sight, hearing, touch, taste, and smell). Intuition, psychic ability, prophecy, and spiritual communication are all done through these energy fields.

When you understand the significance of energy, how it is the core of who you are, and how it is used it to communicate with everything around you, the many Bible verses referring to light will take on a new meaning.

- "The lamp of the Lord searches the spirit of a man, it searches out his inmost being" (Proverbs 20:27).
- "Then your light will break forth like the dawn, and your healing will quickly appear" (Isaiah 58:8).
- "Therefore, if your whole body is full of light, and no part of it dark, it will be completely lighted, as when the light of a lamp shines on you" (Luke 11:36).
- "God is light; in him there is no darkness at all" (1 John 1: 5).
- "Your eye is the lamp of your body. When your eyes are good, your whole body also is full of light. But when they are bad, your body also is full of darkness" (Luke 11:34).

As you release the fear-based, dense, low-vibrating frequencies in your system and replace them with the positive, light, high-vibrating frequencies of love, you will become more unified in who you are and in your relationship with God and with everyone and everything around you. Those of you who want more detailed information on this topic can read my book *Interconnected by God: Healing for Your Spirit, Soul and Body.*

> *"Science is not only compatible with spirituality; it is*
> *a profound source of spirituality" (Carl Sagan).*

The Oneness of All

All of us have energy fields. These come together along with the energy of animals and nature to create the energy field of planet Earth. This then communicates with the energy field of the universe, which communicates with the energy of the Creator God who holds it all together. Since we are created by God, we are all extensions of who God is. Everything we think, believe, feel, do, or speak creates energetic vibrations that move out into the atmosphere and affect everything around and beyond us on an energetic level. We become co-creators with God. So in theory we are all interconnected with each other and with everything around us. We are all part of the spiritual realm.

This spiritual energy is personal and at the same time universal. It is the giver of life. Your spirit is conscious enough to support, protect, and heal you in every moment. It keeps your heart beating hundreds of thousands of times per day, creates more than sixty million cells every minute, and organizes hundreds of thousands of chemical reactions in each cell every second. This spirit is also the intelligence that creates supernovas in distant galaxies, keeps the planets rotating around the sun, and makes sure the flowers bloom. It is the very presence of God that resides within each of us and in all of creation.

Energy never dies, but it can change form. Energy that exists in its unmanifested state is called potential energy. Energy does not discern right from wrong and can be used however people choose, for good or evil. The universe is one interactive system that responds to the energy of your thoughts, feelings, and desires, so focus on the positive rather than on the negative.

Your thoughts are the power used to change your inner being and to change the environment around you. Your feelings help illuminate your thoughts and keep them in place. Picture yourself standing on a spinning disk where only things of the same vibration can join you. Your disk will change depending upon the thoughts you think and the emotions you feel. If you are thinking and feeling happy, you will most likely attract happy people to you. When you look at your life and do not like what you see—sickness, financial lack, or frustrating relationships—you need to examine the nature of your thoughts and feelings. To pray is to change your intention, which changes your vibrational frequency, attracting something different into your life, the things you were praying for. This is why prayer is so powerful and beneficial.

When people perceive themselves as separate from others rather than as connected, they are less likely to pay attention to how their behaviors, attitudes, feelings, and words affect others. When people understand the world from the perspective of energy and see how interconnected creation is, they will often change the way they interact with everyone and everything around them.

- When people comprehend the true meaning of God living within each one of them, they will treat each other better.
- When people comprehend the true meaning of God living within every animal he created, they will take better care of the animal world.
- When people comprehend the true meaning of God living in all of nature, they will take better care of the environment.
- When people comprehend the true meaning of how interconnected we all are, they will pursue peace rather than war, unity rather than separation.

"That all of them may be one, Father, just as you are in me and I am in you. May they also be in us so that the world may believe that you have sent me. I have given them the glory that you gave me, that they may be one as we are one: I in them and you in me. May they be brought to complete unity to let the world know that you have sent me and have loved them even as you loved me" (John 17:21–23).

We Are Not Alone

I have noticed that many Christians fear things they cannot prove through the Bible. For a long time that was how I lived my life, so I never allowed myself to entertain the thought that extraterrestrials and UFOs could be real. However, reading other material about the spiritual realm, I saw enough references to this topic that I decided maybe I should check it out and see if there was any evidence that these exist. I found plenty of books and websites devoted to this topic; they were filled with government and military documentation, personal stories, and scientific evidence. Some of the information I researched came from David Wilcock, John Mack, Steven Greer, Stan Romanek, and Clifford Stone.

In some cultures, people are taught from a young age that the physical world is connected with a spiritual realm full of life and different types of spiritual entities. They are taught that it is normal to have beings from other places visit the planet. In our scientific Western culture, however, people believe that spirit and physical matter should be kept separate and that if you cannot see something with your eyes, it does not exist.

There appear to be many types of alien beings, each with its own purpose, and just like humans, they can be divided into two categories: those that operate from love and those that operate from fear. They seem to be spirit and soul beings like us but in bodies far different from ours. They appear to have been around for a long time, possibly influencing ancient civilizations. The alien races live in many places, some far beyond Earth and others on or in the earth.

Their technologies are apparently far more advanced than what we have on Earth. They travel in a variety of spaceships and can dematerialize their ships and reappear somewhere else. They communicate through telepathy. You can find stories of aliens coming to Earth, kidnapping humans, taking them to their ship, experimenting on them or teaching them their advanced knowledge, and then returning them to their homes. People who claim to have been abducted often say that when they returned they had greater intuitive abilities, felt a stronger connection to all of creation, had a clear idea of what they would do with their lives, and were sometimes vibrating at such a high frequency that it messed with the electronic devices in their home. Other people who were abducted by the bad guys have returned with a great deal of fear.

So why do aliens come to Earth? I found a variety of answers depending on the type of alien being. The good ones are motivated by love and want to help us advance; apparently our science, technology, and communication systems are way behind theirs. They also come to encourage us to be more loving and to take better care of the planet. They see us destroying each other and the planet, and it greatly concerns them. They also warn us of dark forces that want to control mankind.

The bad ones are motivated by fear and come for power and control. Many people believe the illuminati, a cabal, or a shadow government (people use different terms for the same group) is controlled by alien beings. These aliens feed off of fear (just like demons), so they are always looking to create scenarios (war, terrorism, financial collapse, or health scares) to intensify fear in people. If they were to stop doing this, they would cease to exist. So it appears that the more love we can create between each other and for our planet, the more we can reduce the number of bad aliens interfering with life here. The government seems to have a lot of data on UFOs and aliens but fears letting the public have access to this information. A group of people is working hard for disclosure, hoping the government will finally admit these things are real and will reveal the evidence to the public.

Does anything in the Bible substantiate UFOs and aliens? That depends on how you interpret Scripture and how you use your imagination.

- Some suggest that the cloud by day and the fire by night were some type of UFO leading the Israelites through the desert.

- Some suggest the chariot that took Elijah was a UFO.
- Some suggest that visions Ezekiel saw were of aliens or UFOs.
- Some suggest that part of what is described in Revelation could refer to aliens or UFOs.

So why would God create these beings? I do not have an answer for this question other than to ask why not? The more I learn about God and his many creations, the more I realize how little I know. I do know that everything God creates is interconnected through a vast network of vibrational energy frequencies and can communicate with everything else whether human, plant, animal, spirit, or alien. I do not think belief or nonbelief on this topic should split churches or Christians. I admit I was surprised at the amount of evidence I found for the existence of aliens, so even though I could not find solid biblical proof for them, I now believe they could be a reality.

"Perhaps, in retrospect, there would be little motivation even for malevolent extraterrestrials to attack the Earth; perhaps, after a preliminary survey, they might decide it is more expedient just to be patient for a little while and wait for us to self-destruct" (Carl Sagan).

Reincarnation

I was told that as a Christian it was wrong to believe in reincarnation, so I never believed in it or even allowed myself to read about it. From time to time I would come across studies about past-life regression therapy, but I did not accept any of it. But one day the Holy Spirit asked me if we were eternal beings. I said yes and gave the standard answer that when we die we live on forever in heaven or hell. The Holy Spirit then challenged me, saying, "Eternity is a circle that never ends; you have always been and always will be." So where was I before I was born on this planet? Naturally this question led me on a quest to learn about reincarnation. Is reincarnation somehow tied into everything else going on in the spiritual realm? Have you ever experienced any of the following?

- Love at first sight
- Meeting someone and feeling like you have always known the person
- Going somewhere and feeling like you have been there before
- Knowing how to do something you have never been taught
- Children who have artistic, musical, athletic, or intellectual ability way beyond their years
- Children who know things about the past that they should have no way of knowing at such a young age

People attempt to explain these experiences in different ways.
- God has given you a gift—spiritual intuition or the power to prophesy.
- You experienced something that an ancestor experienced or knew.
- You experienced something similar or knew a person in a former lifetime, evidence of reincarnation.
- You are living a parallel life. (I will explain this later.)

Reincarnation is the belief that when God created everything at the beginning of time, every soul that was ever to live on the planet was created. Adherents believe that each person has a higher self that remains in heaven when the spirit and the soul enter a body and live on the earth. They differ over about whether people can reincarnate into animals, plants, or other life forms and over whether they always return in human form. Reincarnation holds that when people are born on the earth a veil is placed on them so they have no remembrance of former lives. If people had this remembrance they would have difficulty functioning in their current lives. However, when babies are born this veil is thinner, and as young children, some could have past-life memories.

There are different theories about what happens to souls after they are created by God.

- All souls remain in heaven until their allotted time to come to earth to live one lifetime, and then they return to heaven or to hell.
- All souls came to earth when the planet was created, and then they died, returned to the spirit realm for a while, and came back to earth for another life in a different historical period. Some people believe they have a choice to remain in the spirit realm or to come back again.
- All souls live parallel lives, meaning they are living many different lives in different historical periods all at the same time rather than in the linear world of reincarnation.

So what is the purpose of reincarnation? Why would you need more than one lifetime on earth? Here are some common theories.
- You need to live many lives to undo the bad karma of previous lives.
- There is so much to experience and learn in a body that you need many lifetimes to experience and learn everything.
- In your first lifetime on earth your soul vibrated at a low frequency. Each time you return you have experiences that

increase your frequency until you reach the pure love that is required to live permanently in heaven.

- God loves his creation so much that he wants everyone to one day be permanently in heaven with him, so he gives you multitudes of lifetimes to find Jesus. When you finally do, you no longer have to reincarnate.

Another way to understand reincarnation is to view earth as a large stage. In each lifetime you get to choose a different character to play, the other actors and actresses, and a story you want to reenact on the stage of life to learn the lessons you need to learn.

Is it possible for us to know what happens when we cross over to the other side and how the reincarnation process works? I wanted to know where people got their information about the process and found that it came primarily from two sources: people who had out-of-body or near-death experiences and people who received the information through dreams, visions, angels, or other spiritual beings. Consulting a variety of sources, I found a similar pattern concerning what happens to people when they reincarnate.

1. *Death and departure.* They float above their bodies and view them and then move up a tunnel of light to heaven.
2. *Homecoming.* They meet everyone they knew who passed on before them. All communication is telepathic.
3. *Orientation.* They are interviewed about how they lived their lives, discussing both the good and the bad, and receive healing from physical traumas.
4. *Transition.* They enter an area like a train station where tunnels lead to different destinations, and they go through a tunnel to meet a group of souls with which they reincarnate.
5. *Placement.* They attend school with other souls and read a life book that tells what they did on earth. They learn how the choices they made affected others on earth.

6. *Life selection.* They look at a screen showing the choices they have for their next life and decide which one they want.
7. *Preparation.* They plan out their future life with the other people in their soul group. They agree on cues (sounds, symbols, signs) so they can find each other on earth.
8. *Rebirth.* They go back through a tunnel and find themselves in their mother's womb for another lifetime on earth.

So does anything in the Bible validate a belief in reincarnation?
- Some people cite the verse that refers to John the Baptist as previously being Elijah.
- Some people note that when Jesus asked the disciples who he was they named people who had lived before as if they naturally expected these people to return and to live another life as someone else.
- Verses refer to Elijah and another prophet returning to earth during the end times.
- Some people suggest that at the time of Jesus, reincarnation was an accepted belief, but the men who chose what books to put in the Bible were more influenced by a Western mind-set than by an Eastern one, so they did not believe in reincarnation and left out any verses or books that mentioned it.

So as Christians, what do we do with the idea of reincarnation? I do not think it makes much difference if we believe in it or not. It is an interesting concept to study and to think about, but I do not consider it something we need to argue over. I do not believe reincarnation determines where we go when we die. However, it could affect the choices we make while we are living on earth and encourage us to live more from love than from fear. While there is plenty of experiential evidence for it, I found very little scientific evidence for the reality of reincarnation.

"Friends are all souls that we've known in other lives. We're drawn to each other. Even if I have only known them a day, it doesn't matter. I'm not going to wait till I have known them for two years, because anyway, we must have met somewhere before, you know" (George Harrison).

Death and Dying

From the day we are born we are all on a journey toward death. Some of us will reach it earlier than others. However, death does not really exist; it is just an illusion since the word *death* signifies a permanent condition. I prefer the term *passing over*. Our physical bodies die, but our spirits and our souls—our energy bodies, the eternal parts of who we are—pass over into the spiritual realm. We are always connected to the spiritual realm in some fashion even when we are living on earth.

We live in a society that does not like to talk about death and dying and will do anything to find a way to extend life on earth even when the quality of that life is minimal. Advertisers spend millions trying to get us to buy things to make us look younger and to extend our lives here. Millions more are spent on medical care, operations, and medications toward the end of life to keep people here as long as possible.

I hope someday we as a society will be able to see death and dying as a normal part of the life cycle and learn how to embrace it with love rather than shun it in fear. When someone is near the end of life, family and friends should gather around to talk, share, forgive, discuss funeral arrangements, wills, and other related information so when the person passes over, everyone feels love and closure rather than regret, fear, or anger. Many times people are ready to pass over but will not because their loved ones have not given them permission; there is unfinished business regarding relationships that need healing. It is important that we who are left mend these relationships and give people permission to cross over, even though we know we will miss them and it may be difficult at first to go on living without their presence in our lives.

The prospect of death is especially challenging when people are young or in middle age and have life-threatening diseases. We want to pray and to believe that God will heal them, but we need to prepare ourselves so if they pass, we are ready. Death is even harder when it is sudden and unexpected and no one had time to prepare for it or to say good-bye to a loved one. This is why every day we should love and forgive everyone in our lives. We must not leave for work or school or go to bed angry at someone. We do not know when our time will come to pass over.

So what is the process of passing over like? I have done a lot of reading on near-death and out-of-body experiences. These are similar in that the body appears to be dead, but then the spirit and the soul return to the body. A near-death experience usually happens when someone is in an accident or on the operating table. An out-of-body experience happens when the person is perfectly healthy, and it can resemble a dream or a vision. What I found fascinating was how similar the experiences were for both groups. Here is a brief description of what happens to people.

- They float above their bodies. If they have been in an accident or have been sick, they feel no pain.
- They can look down on their bodies and see and hear everything that is going on.
- They see a tunnel with a bright light at the end, and they choose to go up the tunnel.
- They feel a depth of love and peace they never experienced on earth.
- They are greeted by loved ones, angels, spirit guides, or Jesus.
- They do not want to return. Some are told they have a choice and do not have to return, while others are told there is no choice and they must return to their bodies.

In returning they do everything in reverse, going down the tunnel, seeing their bodies, and then reentering them. As soon as they are back in their bodies they again feel all the pain of the accident or the disease they had. Those who experienced an out-of-body experience, a vision, or a dream, talked about visiting other parts of our physical world, heaven, hell, or different places in the universe. The people I read about and talked with who have had these experiences all said they never again feared death again.

The other thing I found fascinating was that everyone had a similar experience, regardless of religious beliefs, gender, country, or culture. I was always taught you had to accept Jesus to go to heaven, and yet many people who were not Christians by the traditional definition experienced heaven rather than hell. I looked more into the people who experienced hell. They appeared to be people who denied the existence of God or who were filled with fear, evil, negativity, and other low-vibrating behaviors. If you have a loving relationship with God, there should be no reason to fear passing over. Some people fear leaving their loved ones and the life they know down here. However, from what I am learning when we are in the spiritual realm, we are able to see, know, and communicate with our loved ones still on earth. Remember, everything is connected through spiritual energy, and time and distance do not exist on the spiritual plane.

"Your death? You simply step out of your physical body like you would step out of a garment" (Gabriel)

The Life of a Demon

Having grown up in the Christian culture, I have always believed in the existence of demons, Satan, and hell. However, I have recently discovered that some of my beliefs concerning this topic may not have been accurate. As God has led me into deliverance/releasement ministry with clients, he has given me new insight into what demons are and how to work with them. Some of what I am going to say may shake up your belief system, but due to the positive results I see in clients I now believe it to be the truth.

Two lies can keep you in bondage. One is that Satan and demons do not exist. The other is that Christians cannot be possessed by demons. However, when you encounter Christians who have demons and cast them out, you realize that your beliefs were in error. When we come to know God we bring all of our past and our generational junk with us, and this can sometimes include demons. While our spirits are immediately transformed by God, our thoughts, wills, emotions, and bodies take a lifetime to transform. Anyone can be possessed by a demon; the spiritual laws of the universe apply to everyone regardless of religious affiliation.

Your aura is the energetic shield that protects you from receiving a demonic presence. Any of the following will thin out your aura and make it easy for demonic spirits to enter you: drug and alcohol use, violent or scary movies, books, or video games, pornography, disharmonious music, occult practices, sickness and disease, hanging on to low-frequency energies such as anger, fear, hate, resentment, unforgiveness, depression, worry, or disbelief in God.

I was taught that a demon can be cast out of a person by telling it to go in the name of Jesus. This works, but sometimes the demons return. So I asked God to show me a more effective way to deal with this issue. Here is what I learned. Demons are a very dense, low-frequency energy. When someone passes over, a demon will sometimes appear and attempt to convince the person's soul and spirit to follow it and to reject the light of heaven. People who have denied God or do not feel they deserve to go to heaven are most susceptible due to their low vibrational frequencies. When they follow the demon they end up in hell, and their spirits and souls become encased in demon bodies. Satan then sends them back to earth to possess or oppress people. So within that demon is a spirit and a soul created by God to be eternal. Therefore, it will always have the light of God within it, even if in a minuscule amount.

Now when I discover a demon spirit in someone I have a conversation with it and let it know that it does not belong in this person, that it was tricked by Satan, and that I can show it how to be released back into the light to be with God. Initially the demons are angry and too scared to believe that God loves them. They fear Satan will punish them. When they finally grasp the truth and agree to be released, I ask the demons to look inside themselves to find the light. When they find the light, most are shocked and cannot believe it is in them. I have them focus on it, and as they do it grows larger until all the darkness is gone and they are spirits of light again. We visualize the tunnel of light and invite the angels to come and take the spirit and the soul previously encased in a demon body with them to heaven. The person who had the demon is usually freed of whatever symptoms and problems the demon brought. I do not recommend doing this without training. I have simplified the process to give you a basic understanding of how it works. If you are interested in learning more about this, you can contact me.

We are all spirits and souls who are lost until someone tells us the truth, that we have been lied to and that we are children of a God who loves us and wants a relationship with us. When we choose to believe this, we can look inside ourselves and see the light and the love of God growing within us. Both people and demons are lost spirits and souls until they encounter God and hear the truth. I now believe that some of the Scripture passages that apply to people also apply to demons.

Jesus cast out many demons. Matthew 4:24 says, "People brought to him all who were ill with various diseases, those suffering severe pain, the demon-possessed, those having seizures and the paralyzed and he healed them." Acts 10:38 says Jesus "went around doing good and healing all who were under the power of the devil." I interpret the words *healed them* to mean he sent them to the light of heaven. Other passages say Jesus cast out demons but do not tell us where he sent them. Because of what they have been taught, people automatically assume he cast them into hell, but the Bible does not say this. One passage says Jesus sent them into pigs because that is where they asked to go. (God cannot violate free will.) The uncertainty in Scripture may reflect the fact that people in that culture were not ready to accept the full truth about who demons are, just as in our American culture many people find it challenging to consider a "doctrine of demons" from a place of love rather than of fear. The more we release fear, the more truth can appear.

If you feel like you may have demons in you, the good news is they do not have to stay. There is a way to release them and to set both you and them free. Here are some things you can do to protect yourself and to keep your aura strong enough to resist any demonic presence in or around you.

- Pray to God to cleanse, heal, shield, illuminate, guide, transform, and bless you.
- Form a mindful intent not to be possessed or influenced by Satan and his demons, and reject all that is dark and evil.
- Dedicate your life to God and establish continual communication between you and God through the Holy Spirit, worship, prayer, and other spiritual practices.
- Pray for angelic protection over your surroundings, home, office, car, pets, and children.
- Avoid the things mentioned earlier that thin out your aura.
- Remove as much fear from your life as you can. Fear is the opposite of love and thus will attract the demonic to you.

Many in the church believe that the more you are demonically attacked, the more you must be doing for God or the more God is pleased with you. The idea is that when you are doing something for God demons will come after you with sickness or introduce other bad things into your life, business, or family to try to stop you from doing good. While this may happen, it does not have to happen. Demons obey the spiritual laws of energy. If you are sending out fearful energy, bracing for a demonic attack, thinking that everything in your life is going to fall apart, you will attract demons to you and manifest the very thing you worried about. However, you can choose to do the opposite. As long as you are sending out positive, loving energy, the demons cannot come near you; there is no fear to which they can attach themselves. You might pray, "I thank you, God, that as I go out and minister this weekend, your angels surround me and your love sustains me and pours out of me everywhere I go."

So why would God create Satan and demons in the first place? What do they have to do with love? We always look at Satan as the bad guy. But maybe God created Satan because in order for us to grow and to learn we have to have an opposite to push against, to propel us forward, to compare where we are to where we are going, to encourage us to seek after and become love. Think about how useful resistance is in exercising and building muscles. If you look at Satan from this perspective, he becomes God's servant rather than his enemy. I realize this may be a stretch for some of you to consider; it was for me. You can see this concept illustrated in the story of Job (Job 2, 3) when Satan asked permission from God to torment the prophet. God granted permission but only on his terms. In the end God restored to Job far more than Satan was able to take from him, not just in the physical world but in his relationship with God (Job 42:10–16).

> *"So he traveled throughout Galilee, preaching in the*
> *synagogues and driving out demons." (Mark 1:39)*
> *"And these signs shall accompany those who believe: In*
> *my name they will drive out demons..." (Mark 16:17a)*

Life on the Other Side

Christians love to use the threat of hell to get people to accept the faith. But if God is a God of love, do you think he would approve of using fear to bring people to him? People end up becoming Christians to receive their get-out-of-hell-free card, but they never learn how to have a loving relationship with God, because they see him as someone to be feared rather than loved. Nowhere in Scripture can you find Jesus using fear tactics to get people to come to God. He interacted with people with love and compassion.

So what does one do with all the Scripture verses talking about hell? The answer lies in how we interpret them. We are prone to interpreting verses in a way that supports a long-held belief. When we set aside this belief we can see other meanings within a passage. English translators used the word *hell* to render two distinct and entirely different Semitic terms: *sheol* and *gehenna dnoora*.[7] *Sheol* means to be still or quiet. The ancient Hebrews saw it as a place below the surface of the earth where all the departed, good and bad, remained quiet and inactive while waiting for the judgment.[8] In New Testament times *gehenna* suggested regret, remorse, mental agony, or suffering. It was an idiom that was not meant to be taken literally. *Gehenna dnoora* means "valley of Hinnom," a place outside of Jerusalem where people burned their rubbish and the bodies of plague victims.[9] So the word *hell* was not to be taken literally as an eternal place of torment but was used as an idiom.

It is interesting to note that the few times Jesus used the word *hell* in the Bible, he never said people would go there because they refused to accept who he was and what he taught. And yet this is why the church tells people they are going to hell. Because hell is such a dominant theme for Christians, I thought I would find many passages in which Jesus talked about it. However, I could find only the following verses where he used the word *hell*.

Bible Verse	Aramaic Interpretation of Hell
"But I tell you that anyone who is angry with his brother will be subject to judgment. Again, anyone who says to a brother, 'Raca' is answerable to the Sanhedrin. But anyone who says, 'You fool!' will be in danger of the fire of hell" (Matthew 5:22).	Anyone who says "You fool!" will be in danger of regret or mental suffering.
"And if your eye causes you to sin, gouge it out and throw it away. It is better for you to enter life with one eye than to have two eyes and be thrown into the fire of hell" (Matthew 18:9).	It is better for you to lose one part of your body than for your whole body to be thrown into mental agony or torment.
"Do not be afraid of those who kill the body but cannot kill the soul. Rather, be afraid of the one who can destroy both soul and body in hell" (Matthew 10:28).	Rather, be afraid of the one who can destroy both soul and body through mental agony.
"Woe to you, teachers of the law and Pharisees, you hypocrites! You travel over land and sea to win a single convert, and when he becomes one, you make him twice as much a son of hell as you are" (Matthew 23:15).	You make them twice as corrupt and wicked as you are.
"You snakes! You brood of vipers! How will you escape being condemned to hell? (Matthew 23:33).	How will you escape being condemned to mental torment and wickedness?

I have always believed in the literal hell where people go if they do not accept Jesus. However, while on this spiritual journey, my thoughts about hell have been changing. I believe that God is love, and I have a difficult time reconciling this belief with the idea of people going to hell for an eternity of torture. I realize God does not send anyone to hell. People choose to go there when they refuse to acknowledge him. I also realize that if you do not appreciate God's love on earth you may not want to be around him for an eternity in heaven, so an alternative place has to exist. And if God is really a God of justice, justice would require a place for people who reject him and his love.

We are taught to think of the afterlife in terms of two extremes: heaven or hell. I have another theory. I see the afterlife on a continuum similar to what we have on earth, with a range of people from very bad, evil, and fear-based to very good, kind, and love-based. People always gravitate toward the like-minded. This is because we are drawn to frequencies similar to our own. That is why you will fail when you attempt to teach evil people about goodness. They have no interest in it. They enjoy being evil; it is all they know, so it is normal for them. Love can actually repel them.

I believe the afterlife consists of many communities (mansions) to which souls and spirits go. When you pass over and undergo the life review—or judgment, as some refer to it—everything you ever believed, thought, felt, did, or said will be assessed to see whether it was done from a place of love or of fear. This will determine your true self, and your place in the vast afterlife will be decided by the frequency at which your true self is vibrating. And you will be happy there because you will know this is exactly where you belong based on God's perfect loving judgment. So even if you end up in hell, you will be with likeminded souls, and though you will be tormented in some fashion, you will most likely feel this is normal and acceptable. You will be separated from God in the sense that your location in the spiritual realm will be farthest from the light of God's presence, so you will not feel his love and peace. Those with the highest

Conclusion

When God initially asked me to surrender all of my fears and belief systems to him, I had no idea I would experience as much change as I did. Some of you may be surprised at the conclusions I reached, how I interpret Scripture, and what I now believe. I do not expect anyone who reads this book to agree with everything I have written. However, I trust this book has challenged and encouraged you on your own spiritual journey and helped you understand what "God is love" means for you. Here is a summary of what it means to me.

- Because God is love, I have the privilege of loving all people. Regardless of how much we may be alike or may differ on the physical plane, we are all from the same source; we are all spiritual beings created by a loving God. I found that when I quit comparing, focusing on differences, competing against others, and judging who was right and who was wrong, I could love people without fear. To be able to see God in everyone you encounter is a life-transforming gift.
- Because God is love, I no longer let fear control me. When I begin to feel fear I stop and ask why, where it is coming from, and whether it is a healthy or an unhealthy fear. I ask the Holy Spirit to give me discernment so I can face and release the fear.
- Because God is love, I view church differently. I no longer attend because it is an obligation, something good Christians do. When I choose not to go I do not feel fear or guilt. I realize church is not a building or an organization; it is a group of people committed to experiencing life together, living out the teachings of Jesus in love, and I can do this with people in or out of the church setting.
- Because God is love, I focus on the life and the teachings of Jesus rather than on the doctrines and the beliefs of man.

I evaluate doctrines and beliefs according to whether they are based on fear or on love, and if they are motivated by fear or a desire for control, I will walk away from them. Jesus opposed the scribes and the Pharisees, those who were so focused on laws, doctrines, and beliefs that they missed the law of love.

- Because God is love, I have the freedom to read and to learn from many sources about spiritual truth and about the spiritual realm around and beyond me. I no longer have to fear that I will be stumbling into untruth, because I have the Holy Spirit, whose purpose is to guide me into all truth.
- Because God is love, I no longer have to fear other religions and believe Christianity is the only truth. I realize that every religion has truth and falsehood within it and that we are all searching to find and to connect with the God who created us, regardless of what name we give him. God would never use fear tactics to get people to believe in him. He would use only love.
- Because God is love, I know when we pass from this life to the next all of us will be exactly where we should be based on the amount of love or fear we manifested while we were living on earth. God is a just God, and all of his justice is based on love.

My prayer for each of you is that you will have the courage to identify your fears, to release them, and to replace them with love so you can become all that God created you to be. The more we each make the choice to become a being of love, the more connected we will be to God, the more love will be on the planet, and the better life will become for everyone here. We manifest what we focus on the most. We can focus on all of the war, injustice, poverty, differences, fear, and other negative patterns on earth, or we can acknowledge the presence of these patterns and replace them with the opposite: peace, justice, abundance, our common bonds, and love. I choose the latter and pray others will join me in this choice.

God is love. Therefore, nothing he does can be motivated by fear. I am his child, a reflection of my Creator. Therefore, I will strive each day to live my life motivated less by fear and more by love.

"If I speak in the tongues of men and of angels, but have not love, I am only a resounding gong or clashing cymbal. If I have the gift of prophecy and can fathom all mysteries and all knowledge, and if I have a faith that can move mountains, but have not love, I am nothing. If I give all I possess to the poor and surrender my body to the flames, but have not love, I gain nothing" (1 Corinthians 12:1–3).

Endnotes

Chapter 2

1   Marianne Williamson, *A Return to Love* (New York: HarperCollins, 1993), 91.

Chapter 4

1   Eckhart Tolle, *A New Earth: Awakening Your Life's Purpose* (New York: Plume, member of Penguin Group, 2005), 13.
2   Williamson, *A Return to Love*, 37.
3   Penny Donovan, *Introduction to Practical Spirituality* (Rosendale, New York: Appleseed Publishing 2013), 81.

Chapter 5

1   Thomas Moore, *Writing in the Sand* (New York: Hay House, 2010), 103.
2   Elizabeth Clare Prophet, The Lost Years of Jesus (Gardiner MT: Summit Publications, 1984), 117-119.
3   Nicolas Notovitch, *The Unknown Life of Jesus Christ* (Radford, Virginia: Wilder Publishers, 2008), 57–93.
4   Ibid., 61.
5   Ibid., 63.
6   Ibid., 89–93.
7   Ibid., 57.
8   Prophet, *The Lost Years of Jesus*, 249.
9   Ibid., 259.
10   Ibid., 259.
11   Ibid., 260.
12   Ibid., 261.
13   Ibid., 285.
14   Ibid., 294–97.
15   Ibid., 299.
16   Ibid. 299.
17   Ibid., 300.
18   Ibid., 305.
19   Ibid., 305.
20   Ibid., 305.
21   Ibid., 314–29.
22   Ibid., 325.
23   Rocco Errico, *Let There Be Light* (Smyrna, Georgia: Noohra Foundation Publisher, 1994).
24   Ibid., 13.

25 Ibid., 18.

26 Ibid., 18.

27 Ibid., 19–20.

28 Ibid., 184.

29 Moore, *Writing in the Sand*, 43.

30 Ibid., 94.

31 Daniel Thomas Nehrer, *The Illusion of "Truth"* (Washington: Christian Alternative Books, 2014), 376.

32 Wayne Jacobson, *He Loves Me* (Newbury Park, California: Windblown Media, 2007), 154.

33 Williamson, *A Return to Love*, 74.

34 Donovan, *Introduction to Practical Spirituality*, 34.

35 Williamson, *A Return to Love*, 33.

36 Jarrad Hewett, *The Gospel of You* (New Earth Productions, 2011), 177.

37 Robert W. Funk, Roy W. Hoover, and the Jesus Seminar, *The Five Gospels: What Did Jesus Really Say?* (New York: HarperCollins, 1993), 36, 260.

Chapter 6

1   Funk, Hoover, and the Jesus Seminar, *The Five Gospels: What Did Jesus Really Say?*, 26.

2   Ibid., 6–9.

3   Joseph Lumpkin, *The Books of Enoch* (Blountsville, Alabama: Fifth Estate Publishers, 2011).

4   Marvin Meyer, *The Nag Hammadi Scriptures* (New York: HarperCollins, 2007).

5   Ibid., 133–53.

6   Ibid., 103–32.

7   Ibid., 313–19.

8   Ibid., 321–30.

9   Ibid., 487–97.

10 Ibid., 585–93.

11 Ibid., 737-47.

12 Ibid., 755–69.

13 Helen Schucman and William Thetford, *A Course in Miracles* (Mill Valley, California: Foundation for Inner Peace, 2007).

14 Ibid., 87.

15 Ibid., 44.

16 Ibid. 9.

17 Ibid.,12.

18 Ibid., 12.

19 Ibid., 222.

20 Ibid., 94–95.
21 Ibid., 34.
22 Ibid., 425.
23 Ibid., 31.
24 Ibid., 425.
25 Ibid., 432.
26 Ibid., 666.
27 Ibid., 327.
28 Ibid., 338.

Chapter 7

1 Elaine Pagels, *The Gnostic Gospels* (New York: Random House, 1979).
2 Ibid., 104.
3 Ibid., xviii.
4 Ibid., xix.
5 Ibid., xxxi.
6 Toyohiko Kagawa, *Love, the Law of Life* (Philadelphia: The John C. Winston Company), 312.

Chapter 8

1 Bruce Lipton, *The Biology of Belief* (New York: Hay House, 2008), 70.
2 Caroline Leaf, *Who Switched Off My Brain?* (South Africa: Switch on Your Brain USA, 2007), 4.
3 Dawson Church, *The Genie in Your Genes* (Santa Rosa, California: Energy Psychology Press, 2009), 147–48.
4 Ibid., 159.
5 David Feinstein, Donna Eden, and Gary Craig. *The Promise of Energy Psychology* (New York: Penguin Group, 2005), 199.
6 Lipton, *The Biology of Belief* (New York: Hay House, 2008), 90.
7 Errico, *Let There Be Light*, 34–35.
8 Ibid., 34–36.
9 Ibid., 35.

Printed in the United States
By Bookmasters